CHURCHES WITH ROOTS

After years of decline and the closure of many churches in Europe, some Christians are becoming aware of the possibility of planting new congregations. Here is a book on how to go about this task of change. It comes from a man who has known the pains and joys of bringing churches into being. Johan Lukasse is to be congratulated for combining vision with the practical reality of church planting.

David Burnett, author of
Unearthly Powers and *Clash
of Worlds*.

Churches
with Roots

JOHAN LUKASSE

translated by

Machteld Stassijns

STL Bromley

MARC

Cover design by W. James Hammond

British Library Cataloguing in Publication Data

Lukasse, Johan
 Churches with roots.
 1. Christian church. Evangelism
 I. Title
 269.2

 ISBN 1–85424–087–0 — MARC
     1–85078–073–0 — STL

Co-published with the Belgian Evangelical Mission

STL Books are published by
Send The Light (Operation Mobilisation),
PO Box 48, Bromley, Kent, England.

Printed in Great Britain for
MARC, an imprint of Monarch Publications Ltd
1 St Anne's Road, Eastbourne, E Sussex BN21 3UN by
Courier International Ltd, Tiptree, Essex
Typeset by Watermark, Hampermill Cottage, Watford WD1 4PL

Dedicated to my loving wife, Lilli

Contents

Foreword

Johan Lukasse is eminently qualified to write on the subject of church planting. He has been actively engaged in planting churches for twenty-five years, initially as a Pastor, then as a Field Director, and for the past few years as the President of the Belgian Evangelical Mission.

The experience of planting churches in Belgium has much to teach us about the same task in the British Isles and throughout the world. Most of the issues raised and discussed are general and universal in application. Specific issues are also addressed that relate to our common European context of a nominally Christian and secularised society.

In this book Johan shares his convictions which are based on considerable experience, prayerful reflection, and honest evaluation of churches planted by himself and others. He has not written for 'professionals' but for all who want to advance the kingdom of God and the expansion of the church. For those who are serious about accepting his challenge to plant churches there is practical advice on how to start as well as much wise counsel on principles and methods. For those who feel stuck in a dead or dying church, Johan has good advice. And he is not afraid to suggest radical tests as well as solutions.

Johan constantly uses Jesus and the apostles as models, and the great strength of his teaching is the stress on spiritual realities and the role of the Holy Spirit in church planting. The importance of discovering the receptive, sensitively evangelising them, and co-operating with other Christians is helpfully addressed. I found his major emphasis on love as the means of reaching the lost both compelling and deeply challenging.

There is much in this book to teach the practitioner and stimulate the theoretician. This book will inspire and encourage all who want to plant churches in the United Kingdom, and there are many. England, Scotland, Wales and Northern Ireland are now being seen as ripened mission fields and many bold plans for church planting are being drawn up by denominations and other groups. I welcome this book as a significant contribution to this vitally important means of reaching our peoples with the gospel and bringing our nations to Christ.

The Revd Dr Roy H. Pointer
Director for Church Training
The British and Foreign Bible Society

Introduction

Now that this book is being published I feel like the preacher who gave a lecture about pastoral work. An interested listener came up to him afterwards and asked how long he had taken to prepare the lecture. 'Twenty-five years,' he answered. It was the result of a lifetime of experience.

You could consider this book about evangelism and church planting in the same way. It is the result of working for many years with varying degrees of success. Sometimes the work progressed by leaps and bounds and we began to think we had mastered the technique. At other times, it did not go so smoothly, and problems built up. Through all this God taught us the many lessons that you will find on the following pages. Above all, He made us conscious of the fact that church planting and church growth are under the lordship of Jesus Christ. That is why you will find Jesus' words in Matthew 16:18, 'I will build my church', in almost every chapter. When we are successful in our work for the Lord, it is because He blesses us and not because we are clever. I believe that hearing and obeying the voice of the Lord is the best method for evangelism today. This requires an active faith. By this, I mean that we trust God to be active today; to go on saving people, rescuing them from a lost world; to fill people with His Spirit and enable them to build, nurture and lead His church. What matters most in today's post-Christian Europe is that we should live in awe of God's greatness and not of the Enemy's power.

It is my heartfelt wish that many will read this book. It is not written for professionals, although they might find some of my suggestions useful. With this book I would like to encourage the many Christians who want to get involved in evangelism, and planting and building up the church of Christ, and tell them, 'It can be done!' I have tried to communicate what I have to say in an *inspiring* way. Nothing is impossible with God. When the prophet Elijah lamented, 'I have been very zealous for the Lord God Almighty . . . . I am the only one left, and now they are trying to kill me too,' the Lord replied, 'Yet I reserve seven thousand in Israel—all those whose knees have not bowed down to Baal and all whose mouths have not kissed him' (1 Kings 19:14, 18). God is active in our time as well. More than ever, we need to have faith and trust that God's power and His love for sinners are as strong as ever before.

I would like to thank the many people who encouraged me to share my experience and ideas with you, and assisted in the process. I am grateful to M. George Winston and Dr Theo Kunst for reading the script and offering many valuable suggestions. Although not responsible for the final product, they made a vital contribution. Special thanks go to David and Janet Heywood who edited the text with the English reader in mind. The end result is very much the product of teamwork, and expresses what the church of Christ is meant to be: a fellowship of people saved by Christ's precious blood, following Him and serving one another.

Johan Lukasse
Brussels 1989

PART I

1

Europe in Need

The train from Brussels to Hasselt was crammed full, not a seat to be found. So I tried to read standing up and make good use of my travelling time. My book was entitled *God Can Be Trusted*. Since I am rather tall, a person sitting down could easily read the title by looking up. One man did precisely that and suddenly he read out loud, raising his voice so that everybody could hear: 'God can be trusted. Huh!' All the passengers looked up. 'Are you a priest or something?' the man asked in a loud voice. 'No, I am not,' I answered. 'Why are you reading a book like that then?' he inquired. This started a conversation which held the attention of the entire railway carriage. Here was an interested audience to talk to about the God you can trust.

The striking thing about this was the man's question. If I had been a priest, it would have been acceptable to read a book with a title like that, but I looked like an ordinary person. This illustrates what Os Guinness has called the privatisation of Christianity.[1] By that I mean that Christianity is removed from the public sector, and is tolerated merely as a private interest. Priests or pastors can be involved with it, but not 'normal' people. This is the situation in which Europe finds itself—the post-Christian era, as Francis Schaeffer called it.

Post-Christian

Christianity has lost its significance for most Europeans. The situation is more serious than we like to think. Europe has become a mission field par excellence. Whereas in some countries of Latin America the church of Jesus Christ is growing faster than the population growth rate, in our continent of Europe it is on the decline. 'There's still a strong Christian memory in our Western society. But the main belief today is no longer Christian but humanist—man is putting himself at the centre of all things.'[2] The emphasis is more and more on Christianity as a memory, a thing of the past. If you want to move with the times, you can no longer embrace a Christian philosophy of life. It is hopelessly out of date.

Harry Blamires, in his book, *The Christian Mind*, describes the dominant element of the modern Western world-view as secularism. 'To think secularly,' he writes, 'is to think within a frame of reference bounded by the limits of our life on earth: it is to keep one's calculations rooted in this-worldly criteria.'[3]

Strikingly, Martyn Lloyd-Jones says exactly the same thing about the pagan Gentiles in his *Studies in the Sermon on the Mount*: 'Their view of life is entirely limited by their own thoughts, and they lack this light that is given from above.'[4]

So, secularisation is a modern form of paganism. To recognise this is not easy, as we have become so accustomed to it. This humanist philosophy of life is tantamount to existentialism, which, popularly translated, means: it is not so much whether you arrive or not that is important, but rather what you experience along the way. These are the ideas and interests of most people in Europe today. 'Modern man lives on a diet of "news on the hour, every hour"—almost as if he needed constantly to know that the world was still there.'[5]

This can be seen in what does or does not happen in the established churches:

Where in church the emphasis is no longer on Jesus and is redirected towards other subjects, however unobjectionable in themselves, the church and its leaders have failed. This is the case even though these subjects include a sense of community in the humanist sense or cultural activities or clubs whose purpose it is to offer entertainment and information. Having fun then takes the place of the one vital element. The vitality of the flock diminishes, and the Shepherd's role becomes uncertain, because the attention has been diverted from Him.[6]

Social activity and occupational therapy can never replace the power of the risen Lord. As a consequence, churches have dwindling membership rolls and church attendance is decreasing dramatically.

MARC Europe's report, *Towards 2000,* is very frank in this regard: 'The only continent in the world in which the church is declining is that of Europe which is losing nominal Christians to the cults and sects and various other influences such as secularism and materialism in large numbers annually.'[7] A numerical loss of this kind does not show at first but, when it gains momentum, the snowball effect may be difficult to check. The report goes on to say, 'Whilst the downward trend in the 1970's was small in overall terms it accelerates sharply during the last twenty years of the twentieth century. A 2% decline between 1970 and 1980 grows to a 10% decline between 1980 and 2000.'[8] These statistics apply to Western Europe. The 'church' as a Christian institution is in decline. Numbers are dwindling and although the statistics may vary from country to country, they nevertheless show an unmistakable trend in Europe as a whole. The following paragraphs show more of these unsettling trends.

'Between 1970 and 1980 the British churches lost 1,000,000 members, 2,500 ministers, and closed 1,000 churches.'[9]

Rolf Scheffbuch in West Germany writes, 'It is expected that by the year 2030, the membership of Protestant churches in Germany will be only 50% of what it is today because of the low birth rate and abortion. France might be the worst country with regard to the church—only 1% of the population are real believers. Maybe Belgium is worse. You have to realize that it is a situation that is worse than India or Thailand.'[10]

As to the Netherlands, *The Dutch Christian Handbook* presents the same picture. It discusses the percentage of Christians among the Dutch and suggests a figure of 6,200,000 or 53 per cent of the population belonging to a Christian church or fellowship: 'This percentage, however, is decreasing; it amounted to 61% in 1975 and to 57% in 1980—an average decrease of 1.3% a year, which represents a membership decrease for the church of 150,000 adults a year.'[11]

At the General Synod of Belgian bishops, the Catholic Church's loss of influence and dwindling church attendance has received particular attention. In the conference report it is pointed out that 'This decline is felt in all three of the country's regions but especially in Brussels where Sunday observance has dropped from 20.45% in 1967 to 10.47% in 1979, which represents a relative decrease of 48.80%.'[12]

Further on in the same report it is pointed out, 'But there is a much more significant fact: the relative decline in the percentages of baptisms. These figures are even lower when we consider immigrants from Catholic countries.'[13] There is not only a drop in membership but also a lack of vitality and growth: 'On average it was taking four church members five years to convert just one person. Even in the so-called growing churches, on average, no more than 16 people were being won for Christ in a five-year period.'[14]

If we examine these figures and percentages we can see where we are heading. The situation is dramatic. It is time for us to be concerned, ask for God's forgiveness and take action under His guidance.

Loss of Influence

Of course, numerical loss is not the only loss; the church is suffering a loss of influence as well. Monica Hill writes, 'There is a recognition that Britain is no longer the Christian country it once was: attendance and membership counts have revealed the low degree of importance the British, as a whole, place on "their faith". Christians can no longer bury their heads in the sand feeling that they can still exercise influence in society.'[15] The effect of salt and light which the church of Christ should have in this world is decreasing in Europe today. Moral values are shifting: 'Abortion in Britain alone has deprived the population of over two million children in the last 15 years.'[16] As long as twenty years ago, E. Stanley Jones wrote:

> When a Russian author argued, 'Europe has lost Christ and it will have to perish,' he was not just using a pious phrase, but recording a sombre historical fact. Europe lost Christ the moment it proclaimed Mammon to be her God, even though it still held on to Christ as a figurehead. The only hope for Europe is that from its ashes a humble and purified Europe that is crucified and Christian will arise. Then Europe will be saved; otherwise, it will be lost.[17]

This is prophetic language and we had better pay attention. Europe is a mission field. We are in great need.

Hope

I have been listening to a song by Garth Hewitt called 'Take me to your leader':

> I was listening to the heartbeat of Europe in despair.
> To a world that gave up believing.
> To a world where no one is there.
> But then I read some St. Augustine and found a world that wore a smile.
> It took away my breath and made me stop for a while . . . and I said:
>
> Take me to your leader who has changed you so much.
> Take me to your leader who has that healing touch.
> Take me to your leader who can change a mind like yours.
> Take me to your leader who can open up locked doors.[18]

Seeing Europe in need, Garth was inspired by the miraculous

about-turn in the life of St Augustine. His conclusion is that there is hope. Take me to your leader who can change a godless mind like yours into an instrument for the kingdom of God.

Even better, let us recall the Old Testament vision of Ezekiel 37, in which the prophet is taken to the valley of dry bones. First, the prophet is led all around the bones. Obviously, it is God's intention to convince him that they are really dead and completely dry. Then the prophet is asked, 'Son of man, can these bones live?' That is God's question. The prophet is a wise man and lets God supply the answer: 'O Sovereign Lord, you alone know.' Two things have to happen. God's word must be preached and wind has to breathe into the dead.

Then the miracle happens, they come to life and stand up on their feet, 'a vast army'. All of this concerns the house of Israel, the Bible says, but is there not a lesson in it for us as well? Is this not exactly what needs to happen in Europe today, in her hour of barrenness and spiritual death? Surely God's word needs to be proclaimed more than ever before and we need a powerful moving of God's Spirit, so that the dead can come to life and the dry bones be joined together to become a vast army?

The local church

Even now, God does not want to let us down. It is as in Isaiah 65:1–2 where God says, 'I revealed myself to those who did not ask for me; I was found by those who did not seek me. . . . All day long I have held out my hands to an obstinate people.'

God reveals Himself in many ways: in nature, in Jesus Christ, in Holy Scripture. But since Pentecost the church has been the instrument through which He has been active in this world. This universal church becomes visible when local believers join together. God wants to be active through the church. It is His instrument to make His word and plans known to the world. The fifth book of the New Testament is usually called 'The Acts of the Apostles', but would it not be more appropriate to call it 'The Acts of Jesus Christ through His Apostles'? For, in the final analysis, that is what happened and that is the story that Luke wanted to tell us. Christ rose from the dead; He is alive and active. The words and deeds of the apostles and disciples testified to that.

What Europe needs today is a living, powerful, Christ-centred church; churches through which the risen Lord is at work and which He uses as His instrument to make known His plan of redemption. This plan is presented infallibly in the Bible.

It is vital that we come to a true understanding of God's plan for the local church. Only when we have a clear picture of that can we concentrate our efforts on expanding and increasing the number of churches. In Acts 2 we find a blueprint of how the church should be. Not all the details are discussed, but we find all the basic elements mentioned: 'Those who accepted his message were baptised, and about three thousand were added to their number that day. They devoted themselves to the apostles' teaching and to the fellowship, to the breaking of bread and to prayer' (Acts 2:41–42).

Four elements receive special emphasis: teaching, fellowship, the breaking of bread and prayer.

1. The church is more than a school

The disciples, as the early Christians were called, devoted themselves to the apostles' teaching. There are two points to be drawn from this: first, they were continually learning new things. They never tired of it. You may be sure there was some repetition in the teaching they received, especially since Peter tells them after a while, 'I think it is right to refresh your memory' (2 Pet 1:13). All the same, they persevered. They were eager to learn more and to come to a better understanding of God's plans. Second, it meant that they put what they had learned into practice. They had heard the teaching, and persevered in the practice of it, even though it was difficult at times. And difficult it certainly was. Before very long their leaders were imprisoned and the lives of all of them were threatened. A special prayer meeting was needed and they called upon God to 'consider their threats and enable your servants to speak your word with great boldness' (Acts 4:29). That was persevering in the application of the teaching they had received.

The story, of course, highlights one aspect only, but the apostles' teaching affected all aspects of their everyday life. One thing is certain: the disciples did not learn just to go on living as they had done before; they did not acquire a quantity of pleasing and useful knowledge, which had no effect on the rest of life. On the contrary, it was revolutionary teaching that showed how to live according to the principles of Jesus Christ and the kingdom of God. This teaching, always alive with the power of the Spirit, turned these people into totally different citizens. The teaching is like work done on a house which was originally declared unfit for habitation. After renovation, it is declared fit for habitation. This kind of church has something to say; in the same way, it will make itself heard in post-Christian Europe today.

2. The church is not a monastery

The disciples also devoted themselves to fellowship. 'Fellowship' is one of those rich New Testament words you always feel lose part of their impact in translation. *Koinonia* means 'to share together', 'to own things in common and to exchange them'. People were givers and receivers at the same time. This affected all aspects of life. They partook together of one salvation in and through Christ, that is to say, they all shared one life, the life of Christ. Peter says later in this regard that we 'participate in the divine nature' (2 Pet 1:4). It was a spiritual sharing together, an exchange of what this new life meant to them. They told each other how great and good God was in their own experience. It was not a sterile head knowledge; it was real-life experience. When one felt discouraged, another could help him back on his feet and give encouragement.

But fellowship also involved a sharing of goods. They lived their faith in a very practical way. They took care of each other. They were real brothers and sisters to each other. Not only were their joys and sorrows shared, but their possessions too; they gave to anyone who was in need. This was a testimony in itself, so that it was said, 'See how they love one another.' In short, the Christian community was not like a monastery. No hiding behind a thick wall to be separate from the world. On the contrary, being a disciple meant being completely different, while still being in the world. The disciples radiated a wonderful testimony: 'No one else dared join them, even though they were highly regarded by the people' and 'the Lord added to their number daily those who were being saved' (Acts 5:13; 2:47).

3. The church is more than a distributor of sacraments

There were two clear ordinances which the disciples observed: baptism and the breaking of bread. Christian baptism is a once- only event: 'Those who accepted his message were baptised' (Acts 2:41). By this means they joined up with the disciples. It is a remarkable fact that in Acts 2 no mention is made of exceptions to that rule. We may reasonably expect that the three thousand converts also included those baptised by John the Baptist. All Jews and proselytes, moreover, had been circumcised in accordance with Old Testament ordinances. So a number of them must have been circumcised and baptised with John's baptism. Now all of them were baptised in the name of the Lord Jesus, that is, by his authority in the name of the Father, the Son and the Holy Spirit.

This event turned them into disciples, because it was the first step in obedience to the gospel which had been preached. They responded to the call of Jesus of Nazareth, the risen Lord. From that moment onwards they no longer belonged to the world, but to Him. That was the true significance of their baptism. They had become one with Him in death and had been raised with Him; raised to a new life which they were privileged to live no longer for themselves, but for God (see Romans 6:4–5). They were baptised in the body of Christ and by their baptism in water they openly demonstrated their obedience to Christ.

The second ordinance was the breaking of bread, something the disciples did regularly. The Bible does not offer any specific indication as to how often this was done. Some believe it was daily, others say it was every first day of the week in order to celebrate Jesus Christ's resurrection from the dead. Scripture remains silent about the exact frequency, but *does* indicate, however, that the disciples devoted themselves to the breaking of bread, so they must have done it frequently. It was a celebration in memory of Jesus Christ's substitutionary death and in anticipation of His return. Christ gave this ordinance to encourage and strengthen His church during its existence in between two great redemptive events, namely Jesus Christ's death for our sin and His coming again in glory.

The breaking of bread is a material proclamation: whoever takes part in it, proclaims, 'As I partake of this bread, so I partake of Christ. As I drink from the cup, so I drink from the salvation that is in Christ through the pouring out of His blood.' That is a celebration. More particularly, a joint celebration, for inasmuch as I proclaim to partake of Jesus and my brother next to me proclaims to partake of Jesus as well, we stand united with each other in Him. That is to say, we share the same bread.

We are not to be cut off from real life, having only a mystical value that is incomprehensible to those who are preoccupied with daily life. It is in daily life that these ordinances become so meaningful. They are drawn straight from real life and speak with great conviction about the life we have in Him. When disciples of Jesus Christ go out radiantly into this world, confident in what they are and have in their Lord, they will be very convincing.

4. *The church is not a transcendental meditation club*

'They devoted themselves to prayer.' Prayer is the gift of God by which we can enter into contact with our Creator, the almighty and only eternal God.

Until we have become disciples of Christ, it is hardly possible to understand what prayer is. As the Gospel of John puts it, 'We know that God does not listen to sinners' (Jn 9:31). This means that up to the moment of conversion we can only ask to be forgiven and in so doing become children of God and receive, among other things, the privilege of prayer. In common usage, prayer has been reduced to receiving something in a supernatural manner, at the lowest possible price. The true meaning of prayer is that we gain access to a wonderful fellowship with our heavenly Father. In Christ we are like prodigal sons and daughters who have come home, and His Spirit in us says, 'Abba Father, my Father' to the Almighty. This intimate and personal relationship with Him is a source of power and refreshment.

This is certainly not the contemplation of eternal nothingness! On the contrary, prayer means being in touch with the Creator of heaven and earth. To a Christian, it is like breathing. It is his connection to the power station which generates the energy that he needs to live a Christian life. There is room for both personal and group prayer. The powerful results of the first disciples' faith were due in part to their devotion to prayer.

Today we need prayer more than ever. Church history shows that all upsurges of spiritual life, the so called revivals, started with sustained prayer:

The great revival that swept the Hebrides in the early 1950s through the ministry of Duncan Campbell began with the prayers of those two elderly sisters Peggy and Christine Smith . . . . They had been unable to attend public worship for many years so their cottage had become a meeting-place with God for revival.[19]

When the church is convinced of the needs of Europe, it should devote itself to prayer more than ever before. Jonathan Edwards called for a concerted effort in prayer and soon afterwards a great revival broke out.

Living churches

The church represents the fulfilment of Jesus Christ's promise to us: 'I will build my church, and the gates [or "authorities"] of Hades will not overcome [or "impede"] it' (Mt 16:18). The work of the risen Lord, now sitting on His throne, started at Pentecost. Jesus taught the principles of the kingdom of God: that the other person is more important than myself, and that I am to grow in love. These principles go hand in hand with fellowship, which can only become a reality through the power of the Holy Spirit. Prayer and the breaking of bread are faith-building and festive occasions. This total experience of teaching, fellowship, breaking of bread and prayer sets the church apart from society. It was said of the disciples that they had a new King—Jesus (Acts 17:7). He had become their Saviour and they were living according to His instructions. In so doing, they had become His 'representatives'. The church is both privileged and obliged to make visible the invisible Jesus, 'It is a society of the highest order.'[20] And 'although the church is not to be identified with the kingdom, it should act as a sign and anticipation of heaven's joys and blessings.'[21] Andrew Kane believes that 'the most biblical definition is to say the church is a community of God's people.'[22] In chapters 11 and 12 we shall look more closely at the greatness of the local church as God means it to be. At this point suffice it to say that Jesus promised power, *dunamis,* to be His witnesses.

By this He did not necessarily mean that we are to do door-to-door evangelism, but rather that by His power we can live in such a way that we are His witnesses, *His* witnesses, as His power works in us by His Spirit. This makes the church 'a body of people moving together to a specific goal, as well as increasing their numbers along the route.'[23] What we need is churches that are alive. In all our cities we need groups of believers leading a new life and living out the principles of a New Testament church today.

We need churches in every community. If necessary, we should plant them, by the grace of God and under His leadership. 'Any community of people without an accessible church . . . is a mission field,' declares David J. Hesselgrave, and he goes on to say that 'it is the responsibility of believers in existing churches to fill those spiritual voids with believing congregations. As has often been remarked, neither a missionless church nor a churchless mission is in accordance with the plan of God.'[24] So the gospel must be preached with the intention of planting churches which then pass the gospel on to others.

There is more than one way of achieving this. As Francis Schaeffer has put it:

> My primary point as we prepare for the end of the twentieth century is, on the one hand, that there is a place for the institutional church and that it should maintain the form commanded by God, but, on the other hand, that this also leaves vast areas of freedom for change . . . anything the New Testament does not command in regard to church form is a freedom to be exercised under the leadership of the Holy Spirit for that particular time and place.[25]

Is this the right time?

When we see the true state of Europe in spiritual terms, we have to ask ourselves: Has the time not come for God to act? Should we not be purified again and rededicate ourselves to building His church and to proclaiming salvation in Christ alone?

There are, of course, some encouraging signs and events in Europe, contrasting with the discouraging situations outlined above. Here and there the wind is rustling through the treetops. We can see 'a cloud as small as a man's hand' (1 Kings 18:44).

The total picture, however, remains sombre. The majority of people have a secular frame of mind, with humanism as its philosophy of life and materialism as its ethical code. Existentialism, the here and now, is the only thing that counts. As Wimber has argued:

> In the final analysis, materialism and rationalism are big lies, incapable of providing plausible explanations for meaning in life. The secular world view fails to satisfy people's need to understand the universe, so they look for that meaning elsewhere, even in irrational philosophies and religion.[26]

At a certain point man comes to recognise that he needs something higher than himself. That often happens in a non-rational manner, even though man might not want to admit it. His lifestyle and actions, however, are evidence of that. In his book, *The Problem of Wineskins,* Howard A. Snyder argues that, as Bonhoeffer said, '"We should frankly recognize that the world and people have come of age," . . . But was Bonhoeffer right? Has the world really come of age? What kind of world is ours?'[27]

Snyder goes on to draw parallels with the world of the New Testament and concludes at the end of his chapter, 'Now that the world has come full circle and events recall New Testament days in such a remarkable way, there is reason for hoping that a new church will arise having New Testament vigour. A church that preaches the gospel to the poor.'[28]

Work to be done

So, an enormous task awaits the church of Jesus Christ. 'Son of man, can these bones live?' Where does the church of Christ stand? Are we able to rise to the challenge? Are we ready for it?

Humanly speaking, we are not, but this is exactly where faith comes in. What is impossible with man, is possible with God. In John 20 we find the disciples downcast and huddled together. 'The doors were locked for fear of the Jews.' God had prepared great things, but the disciples were lost in self-pity. They had failed and were only able to see the events of the past few days. At this point the risen Lord enters and changes everything. They rediscover their joy and a song of celebration surges up within them: He is alive, everything is possible.

Then the Lord begins to speak and gives them a mission and an authority. 'As the Father has sent me, I am sending you' (v 21). God is in charge. Always listen to Him. Do as He says and go where He sends you. The authority is, 'If you forgive anyone his sins, they are forgiven; if you do not forgive them, they are not forgiven' (v 23). That is the authority to evangelise. God is going with us and He authorises us. Therefore, everything is possible for those who go in His name.

We believe church planting to be of strategic importance in our effort to reach Europe with the gospel. There is no better strategy for spreading the gospel than that which Christ gave us in the New Testament. Donald A. McGavran believes that 'Church planting needs to be taken seriously because the need for new churches is enormous.'[29]

In what follows, therefore, we shall attempt to give an explanation of how this can be done. One thing is certain: God is able to do infinitely more than we pray for or give Him credit for! (Eph 3:20). In this spirit of faith we are ready to set about the task of planting and building up churches.

Notes

[1] Os Guinness, *The Gravedigger File* (Hodder & Stoughton: London, 1984).
[2] Lindsay Tuffin, 'Western Society Is Rapidly Becoming Pagan, Warns Dr Francis Schaeffer', *Buzz Magazine*, April 1980: p 25.

3   John Wimber, *Power Evangelism: Signs and Wonders Today* (Hodder & Stoughton: London, 1985), p 77.

4   D. Martyn Lloyd-Jones, *Studies in the Sermon on the Mount* (Inter-Varsity Press: Leicester, 1978), p 452.

5   Gordon Jones, *The Church without Walls* (Marshall Pickering: Basingstoke, 1985), p 60.

6   Bram Krol, *Onder commando: een kompas voor de gemeente van Jezus Christus* (Telos Interlektuur: Arnhem, 1979), pp 18–19.

7   Peter Brierley, *Towards 2000: Current Trends in European Church Life,* MARC Monograph No. 1 (MARC Europe: Bromley, Kent, nd), p 1.

8   *ibid*, p 10.

9   Roy Pointer, 'Biblical Guidelines for Church Planting from a Church Growth Perspective', in *How to Plant Churches* ed Monica Hill (MARC Europe: London, 1984), p 24.

10 Rolf Scheffbuch, 'Regional Reports', *World Evangelization*, vol 13 (December 1986): p 4. *World Evangelization* is a publication of the Lausanne Committee for World Evangelization.

11 Peter Brierley, *The Dutch Christian Handbook* (MARC Europe: 1986), p 17.

12 L. Voye, 'Sociologische benadering van de hedendaagse godsdienstige situatie in Belgie', in *Bisschoppenconferentie van Belgie*, Dossier VIII, Proclamation of the 1986 Synod of Belgian Bishops (Bisschoppenconferentie van Belgie Persdienst: Brussels, 1986), p 63.

13 *ibid*, p 65.

14 Paul Beasley-Murray and Alan Wilkinson, *Turning the Tide: An Assessment of Baptist Church Growth in England* (Bible Society: London, 1981), p 23.

15 Monica Hill, 'Editor's Preface', in *How to Plant Churches*, p 9.

16 Brierley, *Towards 2000,* p 2.

17 E. Stanley Jones, *Is het Koninkrijk Gods werkelijkheid?* (H. J. Paris: Amsterdam, nd), p 123. My own translation; the English original cannot be traced.

18 Garth Hewitt, 'Take Me to Your Leader', *Alien Brain,* Word Music UK, MYR C1194, 1985. Quoted with permission: Garth Hewitt, © Word UK.

19 Andrew Kane, *Let There Be Life: The Pain and Joy of Renewal in a Local Church* (Marshall Morgan & Scott: Basingstoke,

1983), p 20.
[20] Andre Hofer, 'Gemeente-vorming', Thesis Bijbelinstituut Belgie 1975, p 43.
[21] Eddie Gibbs, *Body Building Exercises for the Local Church* (Falcon: London, 1979), p 41.
[22] Kane, *op cit*, p 91.
[23] Michael Griffiths, *Cinderella with Amnesia: A Practical Discussion of the Relevance of the Church* (Inter-Varsity Press: London, 1975), p 19.
[24] David J. Hesselgrave, *Planting Churches Cross-Culturally: A Guide for Home and Foreign Missions* (Baker Book House: Grand Rapids, Michigan, 1980), p 39.
[25] Roy Pointer, *How Do Churches Grow: A Guide to the Growth of Your Church* (Marshall Morgan & Scott: Basingstoke, 1984), p 115.
[26] Wimber, *op cit*, p 79.
[27] Howard A. Snyder, *The Problem of Wineskins: Church Structure in a Technological Age* (Inter-Varsity Press: Downers Grove, Illinois, 1976), p 25; and Dietrich Bonhoeffer, *Letters and Papers from Prison* (Macmillan: New York, 1967), p 192.
[28] *ibid* p 31.
[29] Donald A. MacGavran and Winfield C. Arn. *Ten Steps for Church Growth* (Harper & Row: San Francisco, 1977), p 92.

2

How to Start a Church

Sitting on a terrace in one of the smaller cities in Belgium I was watching people as they went by. The same questions kept passing through my mind. Where do we start? Which people should we go to? How do we reach them? Will he or she be one of them? Will there be a lot of teenagers or perhaps a lot of adults? Plenty of questions. Depending on God, we had decided to plant a new church in an area unknown to us. We had done some research and had concluded that there was no evangelical witness of any kind in this city or in the surrounding area. A population of more than 15,000 people and no clear proclamation of salvation by faith in Jesus Christ alone, by God's grace alone. According to our own research there was not a single born-again family, not even one person. There was an obvious need for planting a church of the Lord Jesus Christ. As members of the Belgian Evangelical Mission we had made up our minds to do just that. But how do you start?

A few years have passed since then, and if today you wished to attend an evangelical service in that town, you might well find that 120 to 150 adults have gathered there to sing praises to the Lord and worship Him as their Father in Jesus Christ. God gave us this church, and it has a radiant testimony. But how was it all achieved? In this chapter I will share many of the lessons we have learned.

The first step: prepared people

Our efforts to start a new church from scratch were supported by reading the Bible; we wanted to see how Paul and the others went about it. The first principle we came upon was that after much prayer and listening to God's voice, they went out to look for people God had prepared already to receive His message. In Acts 17:1-2, for example, Paul 'came to Thessalonica, where there was a Jewish synagogue. As his custom was, Paul went into the synagogue, and on three Sabbath days he reasoned with them from the Scriptures.' This was one of Paul's strategies.

What kind of people would he have found there? He found Jews and proselytes, people attracted to the things of God. Perhaps some were there out of habit. Others came with a sincere heart, searching for a living relationship with the God of Israel, and yet others had a 'we know it all' attitude. Nevertheless, every one of them was concerned about God to some extent. Paul addressed himself to this group of people and set about proving from Old Testament evidence who Jesus really was. He talked about His death and its necessity, since man is sinful by nature. Then he spoke of His resurrection and in so doing clearly proclaimed the essence of the gospel to people who could be reasonably expected to be ready to receive it.

In the previous chapter of Acts, we find a totally different state of affairs, but the same principle is at work there. Paul and his associates had found it difficult to discern God's will for the remainder of their journey. After Paul had seen a vision of a man from Macedonia, they put to sea and arrived at Philippi, a Roman colony and the first European city ever to be visited by them. The Bible does not give any indication that there was a synagogue. Paul, in other words, could not apply his general rule to start teaching from Scripture in the synagogue. As we read on, however, the Bible tells us, 'On the Sabbath we went outside the city gate to the river, where we expected to find a place of prayer' (Acts 16:13). What kind of people gathered at a place of prayer? People searching for God. Possibly inadequately informed, possibly having all sorts of strange ideas, but open to the things of the Spirit. So Paul, in fact, followed his general rule: start with the people most likely to be receptive.

We find the same principle in the life and ministry of Jesus Christ. As he stands talking with the Samaritan woman at the well, it becomes clear that this sinful woman thirsts after deliverance and forgiveness. At the same time, she is acquainted with the things of God and knows that the Messiah is to come. After discovering who it is that has been talking to her, she goes and tells the whole village, and her witness prepares people for a meeting with Jesus Christ. Meanwhile He is teaching his disciples the following lesson: 'Thus the saying "One sows and another reaps" is true. I sent you to reap what you have not worked for. Others have done the hard work, and you have reaped the benefits of their labour' (Jn 4:37–38). This is what I. J. Fontenot, in his lectures on evangelism, refers to as 'the harvest analogy' which 'is used to illustrate people who were ready to accept Christ as Savior (v. 35).'[1]

In church planting we should always try to maintain the momentum. It is not like a pastor's or counsellor's work which continues year after year; it is apostolic work. As Monica Hill points out, 'The apostles rarely stayed long in any one city. Their task was to preach the gospel, bearing witness to the resurrection of Jesus, proclaiming Him Messiah, baptising the believers, planting a church, appointing local leaders and then moving on from one city to another.'[2] We should envisage such a ministry in these terms. We might well meet people, for example, who enjoy a good discussion but are not really interested. We should not waste our time with them and fail to be available to those who are interested and are sincerely searching in some way.

Later, when a church has been planted, it could spend its time as a local and permanent witness of Christ with people who are fond of discussing religion, but in a detached, non-committal way. Who knows, God might grant them to be touched all the same by the proclamation and manifestation of His love and grace. Therefore, we need not and should not write anyone off as far as the gospel is concerned, but it is sensible and, what is more, biblical, to behave in a thoughtful way. Jesus 'teaches his disciples to spend their time chiefly with those people who are most interested in the gospel. These lessons we find especially in the Great Commission.'[3]

Practically speaking, this lesson is more important than we might think at first. We are inclined to visit our 'contacts' and devote all of our time to the people with whom we have spoken about the gospel. But we need to evaluate these visits. We have to commend them to God in prayer. Do these people really want to know God? Is God's Spirit visibly at work in their lives? Do they take to heart the things said and explained to them, or does the discussion remain an intellectual exercise, an exchange of information? When planting churches we are limited in time. So we have to look for people prepared by God's Spirit in one way or another: 'That's why it is so important that we search for those whom He is drawing. If we look for them prayerfully, we'll find them. And once we have found them, it is relatively easy to interest them in spiritual reality.'[4]

Those are the ones we have to lead to Christ and train as disciples. They, in their turn, will work with us and bring the good news to their friends and acquaintances. First, it is a matter of training a capable core group: 'Start small! Training requires much time and attention. But in the long run this policy will prove most fruitful.'[5]

From our own experience in church planting we have learned how important this is. We once met a man who had studied to be a priest but had interrupted his studies for some reason or other. He enjoyed listening to us and let us talk to him for as long as we liked and were able. This was happening in a city where, to the best of our knowledge, there were no born-again Christians, so we seized the opportunity with both hands. We spent entire evenings in endless discussions.

But after serious prayer and thought we became convinced that this man was a 'time-waster'. So we told him kindly that we would stop visiting him, since there was no clear sign that he was sincerely looking for God. He got very angry and said, 'You are obliged to come and explain things to me. You claim to be sent here to proclaim what you call "the gospel", but I don't swallow everything I'm told, so because you can't win the discussion you drop out. That's not fair.' We explained it was not the discussion that we wanted to win, but him. What was at stake was not whether we were right or not but whether he was saved or not. God's glory was involved as well in that he had to recognise who God is and what He did for us. We also told him we wished to continue to be friends, but wanted to redirect our attention to people who were interested.

Seven years later we returned to the same place for a Sunday service, and to our utter surprise, who did we find but our friend, the former theological student. We soon got into conversation with him and earlier events were brought up. Then we heard his side of the story. 'Yes, I admit I was very angry at the time, when you stopped talking to me. I don't exactly remember why. I suppose it had something to do with my disappointment that I had not completed my degree at the seminary. Anyway, a few years after our first encounter a man who lived down the street came up to me and started to talk about the gospel. So I told him briefly what had happened to me and that you had given up on me. That did not seem to surprise him and he said, "That's how it goes; they must have been short of time. What they probably did was to find others and explain to them the mystery of the gospel and to teach them how to explain it to others. I am one of those. And, you know, we live right here. We have all the time in the world to talk with you and listen to you. Come and join us at the Sunday service sometime; then you'll not only hear, but also see and experience for yourself what the gospel is all about.' So I came and was slowly won over by the love of God. I am very happy to belong here.'

This shows how some people need a lot of time and may be reluctant at first to accept the gospel. To give such people all of your time as a church planter is not very wise and not in accordance with New Testament strategy. When at some later stage a church has been planted, it can freely spend its time on people like that. The first people we win when working in a new area are all-important. Humanly speaking, they determine the future. So we are not only to look for people prepared by God, but also for those who to a certain extent are 'opinion makers'—people likely to influence others and to open doors for us. Talking about campus outreach, James F. Engel and Wilbert Norton suggest the same principle: 'Campus outreach, for example, logically begins with a focus on their campus leader, and the same can be done in an office, afternoon bridge club, or neighborhood softball team.'[6]

The second step: conversion is no luxury

These days the word 'conversion' has definitely fallen into disrepute. I was standing in the market-place with a small bookstand and a sketch board one day, intending to reach people with the gospel of Jesus Christ. After all, I had learned from the Bible that Christ did more of his preaching in the market-place than in the Temple, and I wished to follow His example. I was on good terms with the market inspector and, consequently, he always gave me a good site. Together with a policeman he came to collect the rental fee. He suddenly called at the top of his voice, 'You there, Reverend, see if you can convert this fellow, he certainly needs it.' As he did so, he was pointing his finger at the policeman next to him. Everybody thought it a good joke.

This is how the word 'conversion' is commonly used. Why is that? Some people sense that conversion is necessary, but are too embarrassed to admit it. But for most people conversion sounds ridiculous in today's world. In a world where man has become the measure of all things and where boundless freedom reigns, conversion is out of date. But this sort of ridicule is a deception from the kingdom of darkness. There is great danger that as Christians we have been so conditioned by the world around us that we only use the word sparingly and with great caution. We would rather not sound so old-fashioned. In church planting ministry, as in all other evangelistic activity, it is vital to speak clearly about the need for conversion. Otherwise there is no foundation for the new Christian life.

There are many kinds of foundations. Some people are rooted in tradition, others in humanistic views or philosophies, or in feelings or doctrines or church sacraments. Still others are attached to a sect or even its leader and his teaching. All of these foundations are false; they are unreliable and need to be tested against the word of God, the Bible.

There is little sense in asking people to give up certain habits or actions when it only involves removing the consequences or fruits from a certain root. Picking fruit does not change the tree. The root has to be transformed and then the tree will follow, and the fruit afterwards.

So we have to start in the right place, at the root, the foundation of life. That is what conversion is all about. When Peter spoke at Pentecost, his teaching was so basic and so Spirit-filled that the onlookers were cut to the heart and said, 'Brothers, what shall we do?' There was not a moment's hesitation: 'Peter replied, "Repent and be baptised, every one of you, in the name of Jesus Christ"' (Acts 2:38). This is where we must start. Being born again is a miracle of God.

What does being converted mean? In *Entering the Kingdom* Monica Hill argues the following:

> A true view of repentance would mean a total change in lifestyle, values and commitment. Commitment to God overrides all other commitments and loyalties. We make a U-turn—turn our back on

the world and our face towards God. John's message of repentance, when accepted by the people, led immediately to baptism in water. 'Repent and be baptised.' The tears of repentance were necessary before baptism. Repentance meant turning away from the past and making a new beginning, seeing the whole of life from a new perspective—God's perspective.[7]

There is always the danger of diluting the gospel in our desire to see a group of people come together to form a church of Christ. We weaken the message here and there and wrap it in a package that is acceptable. This is disastrous. We cannot build on another foundation. True, we are to proceed tactfully and not behave like a bull in a china shop. At the same time, however, we should not compromise the gospel in any way. Whether we find it agreeable or not is irrelevant in this respect. What is the truth or, more accurately, who is the truth, is the crucial point here.

The significance of a foundation of conversion has been shown by George Patterson, who writes:

Repentance is something far deeper than a decision. Decisions are made every day, but you only repent once and for all. It is a permanent change wrought by God. We're born all over again. In Honduras we find that when we baptize repentant believers immediately, without giving them doctrinal courses first, we can follow up the great majority and we teach them obedience from the very beginning. They are saved to obey the Lord Jesus Christ in love, and we don't put a large emphasis on doctrine. The doctrine comes! They will learn all their life. This is the error of the American missionary. He manufactures Christians through an intellectual process. He just blindly assumes that if they learn the right interpretation of Scripture, that this is the way that we make disciples. It has little to do with the brain, but it has much to do with the heart and the soul. Make obedient disciples. Then you will see churches multiply.[8]

I would like to qualify that and say that it has everything to do with the *will*, but Patterson might mean just that when he speaks about 'the heart and the soul'. He goes on to say:

> In Honduras we ask each new church member to memorize the following list of Christ's main commands:
> 1. REPENT AND BELIEVE: Mark 1:15
> 2. BE BAPTIZED: Acts 2:38
> 3. LOVE: John 13:34
> 4. CELEBRATE THE LORD'S SUPPER: Luke 22:17–20
> 5. PRAY: John 16:24
> 6. GIVE: Matthew 6:19–21
> 7. WITNESS: Matthew 28:18–20.
> Teach each new believer from the very beginning to obey all these commands. Don't wait for anything. The first few weeks and months of one's spiritual life are the most impressionable; they will greatly determine his future Christian character.[9]

We, too, are in the habit of putting a one-sided emphasis on the intellect. We can endlessly discuss certain tenets of Christian doctrine, whereas Christ asks us to practise what we have learned in obedience to Him. Being converted means to drink from another well, to live a different life. If we wish to see a Christ-centred church come into being, this must be the starting-point for anyone who joins it.

The third step: the growth cell

The next principle is: bring all who are interested together in a cell group. A group like that could exist under different names. Some call it a house group, others a contact group. In Belgium, Roman Catholics speak of 'core groups'. The name should be chosen with a particular target group in mind. How does it sound to their ears? One of our BEM associates works in an evangelical bookshop and invites people to 'a beginners' study'. That goes down well with most. To quote Dee Brestin, 'A beginner's geatest fear is that he or she will be the only one new to the Bible.'[10]

The concept of cell or core groups is very popular. As Eddie

Gibbs puts it, 'Cells are of two kinds: *prison cells,* which confine, and *life cells,* which develop and reproduce.'[11] We are interested in the second variety! There is a definite advantage in starting a cell group at an early stage of church planting, so that Christians and Christians-to-be learn how to relate to the Bible and to each other. In evangelical circles there is very often a strong emphasis on the individual. We have to be converted personally, we have to develop a personal relationship with the Lord. We cannot go to heaven on the strength of the faith of parents or friends; our faith must be personal, and so on. All of this is good and true, but we are to be a church together. We are also called to be 'God's people.' We can show the world we are disciples of Jesus Christ by loving one another with the love He had for us, and this we can only do together.

In a house group there is so much that can happen by the work of the Holy Spirit in the hearts of those who participate. The atmosphere is more relaxed, people feel more secure and open up more easily. When we meet together with people who have just come to know Christ and others who have not yet reached that point, the latter see the fervour and enthusiasm of the new converts. Can there be a better recommendation for the gospel? There is direct contact as well; you do not have to sit still and listen to a sermon. You can interrupt the leader of a Bible study. You can shoot questions at him. He is right there and is not speaking six feet above authority. He is one of us and if we disagree, we are free to say so. Eddie Gibbs has put it this way: 'Intimacy is essential for establishing an atmosphere of mutual trust, to the point where we are prepared to remove our masks.'[12]

At the moment, the ideal setting for Bible study in Western European culture is a cell group meeting in a home. When asked what his plan of action would be if he were a pastor in a large city church, Billy Graham replied, 'I think one of the first things I would do would be to get a small group of eight or ten or twelve men around me that would meet a few hours a week.'[13]

This principle holds true for church planting as well. Start out with a small group and get stuck into the word and practical Christian living. A small group makes it possible to discuss how we have progressed during the past week. We can build up and encourage one another and, if necessary, correct one another. Such a group like that can become a genuine workshop for the Holy Spirit when we let God transform us. Jesus Christ used this method for training His disciples:

> Jesus had no formal school, no seminaries, no outlined course of study, no periodic membership classes in which He enrolled His followers. None of these highly organized procedures considered so necessary today entered at all into His ministry. Amazing as it may seem, all Jesus did to teach these men His way was to draw them close to Himself. He was His own school and curriculum.[14]

None of us can live and teach as Jesus did, but we can obey his commandment to make disciples. Others then have to start doing as I do because I do as Jesus did. Then we shall have to share our lives and not only our teaching. We shall have to let people scrutinise our lives to see whether we live what we preach. History tells us about the effectiveness of close fellowship in small groups. Ray C. Stedman quotes from evangelical history in this respect:

> During the Wesleyan awakening in eighteenth century England, the great evangelist George Whitefield wrote to his converts: "My brethren . . . let us plainly and freely tell one another what God has done for our souls. To this end you would do well, as others have done, to form yourselves into little companies of four or five each, and meet once a week to tell each other what is in your hearts; that you may then also pray for and comfort each other as need shall require. . . . A sincere person will esteem it one of the greatest blessings.[15]

Speaking about the life of John Wesley, Bram Krol says:

Used by God as an instrument in the Methodist revival, John Wesley organised the fellowships that came into being in such a way that much attention was given to small groups. This method contributed to a large extent to the revival. The name 'Methodism' originates from this.[16]

In *The Problem of Wineskins,* Howard Snyder first quotes from Jess Moody and then qualifies the statement:

> Jess Moody says, 'We will win the world when we realize that fellowship, not evangelism must be our primary emphasis. When we demonstrate the Big Miracle of Love, it won't be necessary for us to go out—they will come in.' I would say rather, our emphasis should be evangelism through fellowship, and especially through small koinonia groups. This is coupling love's miracle with Christ's invitation.[17]

Christ wants to plant His church as a sign and symbol of His kingdom which we are expecting; a new order, a new society. He desires that we grow closer to Him and to each other. All this is stimulated by Bible study: 'In addition to "heralding" the gospel the New Testament mentions discussing (Acts 17:2,17; 18:4,19; 19:8) and arguing and debating (18:28). Communicating, then as now, was a two-way process.'[18] It is a fact that when we teach in that way we plumb new depths. Moreover, practical implications can be discussed together. In the words of Leen La Riviere, 'A somewhat longer preparation and spiritual training is better than a quick burst of fireworks.'[19] It yields fruit, fruit that lasts.

The fourth step: making disciples

Making disciples is the next stage in the process of church planting. These stages blend into one another, but for the sake of clarity we shall discuss them separately. It is most important that we have a clear understanding of what needs to be done and how it can be done. How do converts become disciples?

In the first place, we cannot divide between evangelism and making disciples. One cannot be divorced from the other. Even the concept of a two-phased process seems inaccurate in my view. When we approach people with the proclamation of Jesus Christ, at the same time we approach them with His demands. The process of becoming disciples starts as they begin listening to what He has to say. These are the first steps on the way towards discipleship. And they are not the last! That first step and those that follow, when God throws His light on our souls and on His word, lead to conversion. The process of becoming a disciple starts right there:

> We must stop seeing conversion and discipleship as two steps. As long as we see first one and then the other, discipleship will be sec- ondary. And secondary things are often left undone. In our limited vision, it is difficult to tell when someone is actually in the Kingdom. Jesus knew that—and told the parable of the wheat and tares (Matt. 13:24–30). We must work with those who 'seem to believe', not stopping when we think someone is converted.[20]

Dee Brestin goes on to say that 'As long as we don't see dis- cipleship as an integral part of evangelism, those whom we think are won may not be won at all, and those who are won may never be strong enough to win others.'[21] This is straight talking. We should keep in mind that Jesus did not send us to make Christians or to gather a harvest of converts. The com- mand is 'go and make disciples of all nations' (Mt 28:19). James Engel has explained that 'as long as we see Christian growth as a second step, conversion will have centre stage and the result will be a weakened church.'[22]

We should also keep in mind that we turn people into dis- ciples of Jesus Christ, not of ourselves. How did Jesus go about making disciples? In *The Inescapable Calling* R. Kenneth Strachan tells us:

Mark states in a pregnant phrase, 'And he ordained twelve, that they should be with him' (Mk 3:14). This certainly is one key to Christ's method of discipling. The call is 'Follow *me*.' As they observed him in his private life and participated in his public ministry, and as they accompanied him along the roads of Palestine, they were formed into disciples.[23]

They observed the Master's actions and His words, 'Follow me,' did not just mean 'Go where I go,' but also 'Do as I do' and 'Be like me.' We see this in action after Jesus speaks the same words to Levi, 'Follow me.' Levi responded by holding a banquet at his house and inviting all his friends, fellow sinners, and Jesus (Lk 5:27–32). He was doing what Jesus Himself did: bringing sinners to God through Jesus Christ.

The church planter should do the same. In trying to win people for the kingdom of God, he not only passes on the good news, he *is* the good news. This is how Paul acted. When we look at the state of affairs in Thessalonica in Acts 17, we discover that his visit not only resulted in people coming to faith but also in changing their lifestyles to such an extent that it was said they served another King called Jesus. Later on, in a letter to the Thessalonians, Paul wrote, 'You became imitators of us and of the Lord' (1 Thess 1:6). So these people not only accepted the good news but went beyond that and did as Paul did, because he did as Jesus did. In so doing they became followers of Paul and of the Lord.

As a church planter in Belgium I experienced something which helped me to understand this principle more clearly. We started a Bible study in a Christian home, the only one in the area, and invited a variety of people: neighbours, friends, colleagues, whoever wanted to come. Little by little there was progress. Some people came and brought others along. The Bible study was quite an event. We learned some new songs and the word was explained with enthusiasm, accompanied by many lively illustrations. It was applied directly to those gathered and to their daily lives. Some people were converted. Questions were raised and answers were given. We prayed and God answered some of our prayers very clearly. Those who were there when the Bible study first started, and had been converted, brought others along with them. These people came with questions of their own, which often were identical to those others had asked before them. This created something of a problem. What were we to do? Split up the group perhaps? That seemed a little premature.

One evening, some old questions came up again. I prayed an urgent prayer and asked, 'Lord God, tell me what to do. The more advanced ones will lose interest when I answer the questions, but the newcomers need an answer.' The Lord showed me what to do. So I asked whether all present would approve if I finished at 10 o'clock and let those who already knew the answers pass them on to the others. This met with general approval. At the appointed time I stopped and said, 'Some of you still have to explain certain things to the others.' Meanwhile, a number of other questions had cropped up, with the result that nearly all of the first converts had a task.

We followed that same pattern in our later Bible study sessions. From the start it became clear to me that the real work only began at 10 pm. This discovery gave me great joy and happiness and I said, 'This is great, Lord! I am making disciples now!' In fact, these people were doing what I had done before them: helping others find the way to God. It was a day to remember, and the church has grown as a result.

The fifth step: being disciples

When by the grace of God we are able to get through to a number of people, to lead them to Christ and make them into His disciples, they start out on a life of discipleship. As Peter Wagner has pointed out in *The Crest of the Wave*, 'Some have confused "making disciples" with "discipleship." *Making disciples* is the right goal of evangelism and missions according to the Great Commission. Once disciples are made, they then begin the lifetime road of *discipleship*.'[24] In the context of church planting this means that we are to start off a continuing process of teaching and handing over responsibility. Local believers come of age as Christians and begin to carry the responsibility of their church—a very important step.

Gottfried Osei-Mensah of the Lausanne Committee for World Evangelization (LCWE) warns, 'I am concerned that unless we find some way of discipling and instructing the new Christians, we might be in danger in a generation or two, when we have a large body of interested people who call themselves Christians but who have not been taught.'[25] However, training is very different from teaching, and it is training that interests us at this point. So we have to assign new believers to the smaller tasks at an early stage. Pretty soon they are asked, and are able, to contribute to the advance of the gospel and the building up of the church. I do not mean that new believers should just arrange the chairs or do some other duty. It is, of course, good that they do these things in the Spirit of Christ, who served among us. But we should not delay in giving them spiritual duties as well.

Something which has proved effective in my experience is to encourage new converts to share the testimony of their new-found relationship with God as soon as possible. Often I ask, 'Do you have someone very close to you who you would like to know what you know now?' After a moment's reflection, the name of a friend or relative will come to them. Then I say, 'Why don't you go and tell them?' This is when the 'buts' start coming: 'How will they react? What will they say? What shall I say when they start asking questions?,' and many similar excuses.

Then I suggest that I should go with them. Most people like the idea, so we make an appointment and set out together. I am introduced as a new friend. When there is a pause in the conversation, I say, 'Your brother has some important news for you, but he is a little shy about it.' This is the starting-point. There might be some stuttering in the beginning, but when the new convert talks about what he has found in Christ, there is no stopping him. I just keep my mouth shut and pray.

By this method I have discovered the full measure of the power of the Holy Spirit in the lives of the newly converted! I confess I thought at first, 'They don't know enough, they have to deepen their knowledge to be able to do this,' but I was wrong. A new convert does not know very much about Christian doctrine, but that is not what the other person needs at this point—he needs Jesus Christ! Also, this young brother or sister in the faith has not yet acquired the evangelical jargon that we use and that can be hard for outsiders to understand. I have heard people explain conversion and new birth in the ordinary language of the factory and the street, the language that people understood.

When people learn to share their faith from the very beginning, they rapidly gain confidence and play their part in building up others. As time goes on, we can entrust others to their care and guidance. This is the 'elder brother' method. When someone joins us we must receive him warmly and lovingly in our midst but should also appoint an elder brother in the faith to give him special attention.

Later, for example, we could ask certain people to introduce cell group sessions before the Bible study. They could open with prayer and a word of welcome. They could start with a few words about a Bible passage, as long as it does not turn into a sermon. They could lead the personal exchanges and possibly be the first to talk about how they have walked with the Lord in the past week. Later still they could deputise for the church planter and lead a small study. All of this could be done under the supervision of the church planter, who should not sit by and judge like a schoolmaster, but correct and encourage and give constructive criticism. David J. Hesselgrave reminds us in this respect that 'It is a fundamental law of pedagogy that one learns by doing. Learning is not simply a matter of cognition. It is also a matter of action. Learning that is divorced from life, that is only a matter of accumulation of data, is hardly worthy of the name.'[26] Eddie Gibbs confirms this when he says, 'In the church, people are learning, not simply through listening, but by doing.'[27]

We should be far-sighted enough to see a progression from the moment people are converted (possibly through our ministry), through the stage of assisting us, to finally becoming fellow leaders with us. Our ultimate purpose should be that in the future they will take over from us and continue the work. We therefore have to help people learn how to live in total devotion to Christ, and from there to develop an unshakeable trust in Him. We are to teach people how to relate to the word, how to acquire a practical and ready knowledge of the Scriptures and how to put their trust in the power and presence of God's Spirit in their lives. As church planters we should also learn to have faith in God's work in them. We have to be an example, so that they see that we have faith in God who is at work in them. For we, as much as they, have to keep to the path of discipleship.

The sixth step: being a church

There comes a time when we have to appoint local leaders and pass on the torch. The sooner that is, the better. David Burnett believes 'an indigenous church requires a deep trust in the young converts and an indigenous leadership should be encouraged from the very beginning.'[28] If we start with this vision, then our objectives will be clear throughout the process. In the Belgian context, which is rather difficult for church planting, there have been in my experience at least two different occasions when people knew from the start they had no more than three years to complete their assignment and were to hand it over when their time was up. In both cases we succeeded in appointing new leaders before the deadline. Even though things seemed in a delicate state of balance at the time, we took the risk. God responded to our faith and gave us growing churches. It is vital to appoint local leaders in good time; it requires some self-denial on the part of the church planter. But is not this exactly what he proclaims, that we have to deny ourselves and take up our cross and follow Christ?

Peter Wagner has said, 'Many mission specialists believe that leadership selection and training is the single most crucial issue in the spread of the gospel throughout the world today.'[29]. Local leadership will remove the strange and foreign element of the missionary's work. The more the unchanging message of the gospel of Jesus Christ is rooted in local culture and customs, the better. Living it out must have a local flavour. We can expect this to happen when local leaders are appointed.

Once such leaders have been appointed, the time has come for the church planter to leave. New leaders can never develop to their full potential while he is around. More often than not he has a strong personality, so his departure will prevent him from making a little kingdom of his own that would be doomed to disappear. We shall discuss this in detail in Chapter 9, but for now, I simply refer to something Robert Coleman has said: 'One must decide where he wants his ministry to count—in the momentary applause of popular recognition or in the reproduction of his life in a few chosen men who will carry on his work after he has gone.'[30]

The church planter has to pay the price, as well as the others. Naturally we are tied by many bonds of affection, and severing them will be painful. However, as Coleman puts it, 'We are not primarily living for the present. Our satisfaction is in knowing that in generations to come our witness for Christ will still be bearing fruit through them in an ever-widening circle of reproduction to the ends of the earth and unto the end of time.'[31] That is why church planting, if planned and done in the right way under God's leadership, is so rewarding.

Notes

1 I. J. Fontenot, Lecture 3 of 'Biblical Perspectives for Evangelism and Church Development', WEF Ministries Candidate School, Langhorne, Pennsylvania, 1985, p 7.

2 Monica Hill, 'A Biblical Introduction', in *How to Plant Churches* (MARC Europe: London, 1984), p 18.

3 Bram Krol, *Onder Commando: een kompas voor de gemeente van Jezus Christus* (Telos Interlektuur: Arnhem, 1979), p 131.

4 Dee Brestin, *Finders Keepers* (Hodder & Stoughton: London, 1984), p 16.

5 Krol, *op cit,* p 134.

6 James F. Engel and Wilbert Norton, *What's Gone Wrong with the Harvest?* (Zondervan: Grand Rapids, Michigan, 1982), p 99.

7 Monica Hill, 'Entering the Kingdom—Then and Now', in *Entering the Kingdom: A Fresh Look at Conversion,* ed Monica Hill (MARC Europe: Bromley, Kent, 1986), p 2.

8 George Patterson, 'The Spontaneous Multiplication of Churches', in *Perspectives on the World Christian Movement,* ed Ralph D. Winter and Steven C. Hawthorne (William Carey Library: Pasadena, California, 1983), p 610.

9 *ibid*, p 610.

10 Brestin, *op cit,* p 153.

11 Eddie Gibbs, *Body Building Exercises for the Local Church* (Falcon: London, 1979), p 55.

12 Eddie Gibbs, *I Believe in Church Growth* (Hodder & Stoughton: London, 1985), p 169.

13 Robert E. Coleman, *The Master Plan of Evangelism* (Fleming H. Revell: Old Tappan, New Jersey, 1982), p 120.

14 *ibid,* p 38.

15 Ray C. Stedman, *Body Life: The Church Comes Alive* (Regal Books: Glendale, California, 1972), pp 111–112.

16 Krol, *op cit,* p 110.

17 Howard A. Snyder, *The Problem of Wineskins: Church Structure in a Technological Age* (Inter-Varsity Press: Downers Grove, Illinois, 1976), p 42; and Jess Moody, *A Drink at Joel's Place* (Word Books: Waco, Texas, 1967), p 24.

18 Gibbs, *Church Growth,* p 145.

[19] Leen La Riviere, 'Succesvol evangeliseren', in *Evangelisatie,* ed Leen La Riviere (J. H. Kok: Kampen, 1980), pp 12–13.

[20] Brestin, *op cit,* p 167.

[21] *ibid,* p 168.

[22] *ibid,* p 169.

[23] R. Kenneth Strachan, *The Inescapable Calling* (William B. Eerdmans: Grand Rapids, Michigan, 1968), p 56.

[24] C. Peter Wagner, *On the Crest of the Wave: Becoming a World Christian* (Regal Books: Ventura, California, 1983), p 110.

[25] Quoted in Allen Finley and Lorry Lutz, *Mission, a World Family Affair: Sharing Resources in the Church around the World* (Christian Nationals Press: San Jose, California, 1981), p 60.

[26] David J. Hesselgrave, *Planting Churches Cross-Culturally: A Guide for Home and Foreign Missions* (Baker Book House: Grand Rapids, Michigan, 1980), pp 309–310.

[27] Gibbs, *Body Building,* p 56.

[28] David Burnett, 'Cultural Factors and Indigenisation in Church Planting', in *How to Plant Churches,* p 51.

[29] Wagner, *op cit,* p 159.

[30] Coleman, *op cit,* p 37.

[31] *ibid,* p 126.

3

How to Deal with Dead Churches

Everyone enjoys unwrapping a brand new object, and new churches seem to hold the same attraction. They are fresh and full of life, and people are drawn to them like bees to a honeypot. But what can be done about older churches that are more set in their ways?

The need

The question which preoccupies many Christians who are loyal to the Bible is, 'Do I have to stay with my church?' It is so dead. A stale smell hangs over it and the biblical truths seem to be covered in cobwebs. There is no clear proclamation of the necessity of conversion, no teaching on how to grow. People have become set in traditional ways which do not stand the test of the Bible. Other churches are quite different. Everything seems modern, with much attention given to politics and humanitarian concerns so that the message of the Bible is stifled, and its authority is called into question. The Bible is considered the product of another age, its writers lacking the knowledge that we have today. And there are many other kinds of dead churches, too. Many individuals and families face the question of whether or not to stay in their church. It is a question of conscience, and they struggle with it. On the one hand there is the hope that God will give new life and renew all things; on the other hand there is a drifting away from God and His word, until hope is lost and there is no inclination to invite others. This is how Christian lives turn to waste. They have no spiritual point of reference.

Another issue which concerns Christians in dead churches is their financial contribution. 'Where does my money go to?' Some Christians say with Michael Griffiths, 'Should we write Ichabod ("The glory has departed") over all older churches, merely by reason of age, or style of worship, and has the Spirit indeed been withdrawn from us?'[1] We have to face that question.

The key question

Bram Krol wrote, 'When we test the churches against the eternal standard of Holy Scripture, we soon discover that a lot is out of step. What should we do about it? We should not choose the line of least resistance. Sometimes this would just mean leaving the church.'[2] A little later he argues, 'When you work in your church, you have to realise that you will be dealing with old traditions, institutions and sensibilities. New things are not usually encouraged. . . . It will be a test of our love and patience.'[3]

We then ask ourselves, 'Are we not fighting a losing battle?' If all our strength is used up in an internal struggle, what is left for witnessing to the world around us? Of course, every church will be found lacking one way or another; the ideal church does not exist. In 1 Corinthians 3:16, the believers at Corinth were still addressed as 'God's temple', even though a lot was going wrong there. In fact, the whole letter gives guidelines as to how to clear the rubble—how to clean up sin and wrongdoing and return to living in love and purity. The people of Corinth were still on the foundation of Christ, and that is what counts.

I believe we should ask ourselves two questions before we decide whether or not to stay in a church like that. The first is theological: Is the foundation upon which they build still sound? The second is practical: Is there still spiritual life? I find it hard to agree with Bram Krol who believes that 'If every initiative towards spiritual renewal in a certain church is being discouraged, it is still possible to get involved in an evangelical organisation so that with its help you can take part in Bible study and evangelism and encourage others to do the same.'[4] But what will you do then when people are converted and want to follow Christ? Will you tell them they should not join your church because things are seriously wrong there? If we cannot answer these questions satisfactorily, we should look elsewhere.

No foundation

The first question was theological in nature; it deals with the foundation upon which churches build. B. C. Carp observed that 'When churches have been emptied, it is not so much because sermons do not address the actual problems of this day and age. It is rather because they treat these issues to the exclusion of all else and fail to proclaim, or proclaim only feebly, the eternal rock of man's salvation.'[5] This is the heart of the matter. The church is not some kind of social institution whose purpose it is to give direction to society. On the contrary, it is God's instrument to proclaim His word. The cornerstone of its foundation must be: 'This church accepts Holy Scripture as the God-given standard which is wholly reliable and determines all of life.' Otherwise, there is little hope for a church and there would be no sense in our staying there. The words of Psalm 11:3 apply here: 'When the foundations are being destroyed, what can the righteous do?' Scripture is the source of authority and when that is undermined, there is no basis left, however good and holy the intentions might be.

Often Scripture is not rejected as a whole, but rather its authority is undermined in the way it is explained. In *Ten Steps for Church Growth* Donald McGavran and Winfield Arn emphasise the authority of the Bible for all times:

Origen, an early Church Father, explained Scripture away allegorically. Today, some would explain it away anthropologically. They say, 'In those circumstances, in that culture, the Bible meant that; but that is not true for us today.' While it is true that the Bible was spoken to that culture and to those people in those circumstances, it was given for our edification. It was not spoken to that culture only. God revealed his truth for that culture and for all times and all men.[6]

Scripture itself confirms this many times over, but we shall confine ourselves to one passage, from the letter of Jude: 'Dear friends, although I was very eager to write to you about the salvation we share, I felt I had to write and urge you to contend for the faith that was once for all entrusted to the saints' (Jude 3). When a church no longer contends for the faith, it is like a ship without a compass, and had better be abandoned. If the Scriptures are not our guide there will be no point of reference by which to call one another back from a wrong course.

I do not intend to give a list of reasons why one should leave a church; this has to be weighed up in prayer on the basis of the key question. What is at stake here is not a variety of theological opinions that are all Scripture-based. There is room for a whole range of opinions about things of lesser importance, but there is no room for differing opinions about the Trinity, the divinity of Jesus Christ, God the Creator, reconciliation with God by Christ's accomplishment alone, etc.

Concerning the matter of staying with or leaving a church, I would like to put forward two more points to consider. The first is: 'Does the fellowship share the conviction that people who do not know Christ are lost?' Do we need to proclaim the gospel or not? The church's answer will govern its action and its future. As McGavran and Arn point out, 'Intellectually, most Christians and most churches believe that those outside Christ are lost, but does the truth get into every practical aspect of thinking, planning and programming? Many church members tend to see Saviorless and Masterless neighbors and friends as not lost, not condemned, not bound for a Christless eternity.'[7] This gives food for thought.

The second point is, 'Does the church share the conviction that Christ is the only way of salvation?' There is no other way, Christ told us so Himself. In the words of McGavran and Arn, 'No man-made religion offers a way of salvation, forgiveness of sins, peace with God, reconciliation with the Father, and the indwelling presence of the Holy Spirit. Christianity is unique.'[8]

To give up this conviction would mean that we have nothing to offer in this world of need, whereas we have been saved precisely to proclaim God's mighty deeds and salvation, as His own people. A church that no longer flies this flag has nothing to offer and has strayed from God's plan. In that case it is better for us to leave and make our spiritual home with another church for the sake of our personal spiritual growth and our becoming a blessing to others. Naturally, our motives should be pure and not be dictated by the desire to solve personal problems and conflicts.

An empty temple

The second question is of a more practical nature: 'Is there still spiritual life in the church?' There is no sense in holding on to the church as an institution when the Spirit has departed from it. Paul's letters and the opening chapters of Revelation clearly show that God might leave the church, so that only a social club remains. The Lord says to the church in Ephesus, 'If you do not repent, I will come to you and remove your lampstand from its place' (Rev 2:5). When things have come to this, we no longer have a church of Christ. The few real Christians left in such a church 'are like shipwrecked mariners huddled together in a life-boat, sending out their distress signals and awaiting the arrival of the rescue helicopter!'[9] A meeting of people who talk about religion is not necessarily a church. What counts is the biblical principle laid down by

Jesus, 'Again I tell you . . . where two or three come together in my name, there am I with them' (Mt 18:20). Is He present among them as 'the head of the body, the church . . . the beginning and the firstborn from among the dead, so that in everything he might have the supremacy'? (Col 1:18).

Much can go wrong in a church, but when Christ has departed from it, it no longer belongs to Him. The Old Testament teaches us the same lesson. The people of Israel trusted the fact that the Temple was in their midst, but they were living in sin and had strayed from the ways of the Lord. At that moment the prophet Jeremiah comes forward to speak in God's name: 'Do not trust in the deceptive words and say, "This is the temple of the Lord, the temple of the Lord, the temple of the Lord!"' (Jer 7:4). There follows a serious warning not to trust in outward appearances, since God looks at the heart and judges the works that come from it.

In Ezekiel's prophecy the imagery is even more dramatic. God shows the prophet how 'the glory of the Lord' was present in the Temple at first, but could no longer reside there because of the detestable practices that were done in secret. Concerning the people of Israel, 'They thought God was safely within the temple and among the priests, but suddenly he came at them from outside, through the voice of the prophet and in the thunder of foreign kings.'[10] So we should not hold on to externals. The church is where the Lord meets His people. When His life is no longer there, what sense is there in staying? Somebody once told me, 'I left my church some two years after God had left it.' To stay when God has left is foolish, to say the least.

Symptoms

The question we are then faced with is: How do we know when God is no longer there? This question is more difficult. There is the danger of subjectivity. Our feelings often play a greater role than we realise. We then have to proceed with care and much prayer. We may need advice from others. The following questions are helpful in determining whether the church we go to is a church of Christ.

1   Is there still growth? In John 15:2 Jesus uses the image of the vine and the branches when he says, 'He cuts off every branch in me that bears no fruit.' By 'He' is meant the Keeper of the Vineyard, His heavenly Father. Therefore, one way or another, there has to be fruit, however small that may be for the moment. The size of a mustard seed perhaps, but that could grow to be a tree.

2   Is there sincerity? The only people Christ ever talked about without mercy were the Pharisees. 'Woe unto you . . . .' In the early church dishonesty was punished severely, as can be seen in the death of Ananias and Sapphira.

3   Is there variety in leadership? In other words, is there some real spiritual life in at least one of the leaders? Often it is hard to contribute to the revival of a church from the grass-roots upwards, when there is no one among the leaders who can act as a sounding board. Add to this a system where leaders appoint their own successors, and there is little hope left. The people of Israel most often went astray when their leaders no longer obeyed God. After all, there is little chance that a minister or priest will repent by hearing his own sermon!

4   Is there still a genuine concern for the things of the Spirit? Bram Krol points out that 'It is typical of dead churches that a lot of time is given to organisation and administration, leaving no time for spiritual duties.'[11] In other words, there is structure, but no power. This reminds me of Samson who had lost his hair and his strength, and 'thought, "I'll go out as before and shake myself free." But he did not know that the Lord had left him' (Judg 16:20).

No doubt, we could ask ourselves some more questions, but the few I have listed might at least help to put things in perspective.

Leaving the ship

Let us assume we find ourselves in a situation which answers to the description given by Vance Havner: 'Pray for us here. The blower is still blowing but the fire is out!'[12] If we decided to stay, we would then be exposed to certain dangers. Just like the others, we could be overcome by the stench of death and lose our fervour and zeal for the Lord. This usually happens slowly, so you might not notice it. In this context the Bible speaks about 'drifting away' (Heb 2:1). Our spiritual growth and our bearing fruit will stagnate:

> The Spirit initiates felt need by showing the gap that exists between 'what is and what ought to be.' The believer, then, must decide what to do—either to obey under the guidance of the Spirit and appropriate God's solutions or to disobey and, in effect, slump into a stage of arrested growth.[13]

Time is ticking by, and we want God to accomplish His plan in our lives. We want to play our part in building up His church. In some cases, this can best be done by leaving the sinking ship of a lifeless church.

In such a situation, let us tread very carefully. Our reasons for leaving should be thought through honestly and should be made known in talks with the church or its leaders. They might be open to what we have to tell them. They might then understand if no changes are made and we actually leave. When we leave we should not slam the door as we go. We are not called to cause a division. The best thing to do is to inform church leaders of our resolve before we go.

At that point the choice is open to us either to join an existing church or start a new one with a number of Christians who are in the same predicament. This choice, too, should be made after much prayer and with great care. When we believe God has called us to plant a new church, we need to prepare for it carefully. Some advice might be appropriate here, to help us find out how to proceed. What kind of church do we believe God wishes us to help build? Sacrifices will have to be made in order to work everything out in dependence on Him.

Burying death

Many times, fortunately, we need not come to the conclusion that we are fighting a losing battle. To be sure, things could look bleak. Much could be improved if done differently. But there is still the belief that under the ashes of a dead fire the embers are still smouldering. From time to time people are converted and cell groups formed from which new life is allowed to grow. Bram Krol says that 'dead churches may come to life again through a massive turning back to Jesus Christ. This is what happened in a number of revivals.'[14]

More recent examples of revival could be quoted, especially in Great Britain. Andrew Kane suggests where to start: 'Before we can expect new life and resurrection power, we have to roll away the stone and expose what is death to the gaze of Jesus. . . . We learned that, before life can come to the body, death needs to be acknowledged and properly buried.'[15] He goes on to describe their church's 'inner mission'. This was evangelism directed towards the church itself, aimed at self-examination and repentance, in a desire for the new life and strength that Jesus has promised us:

> That night at the inner missions, we were having to do some burying. Only later did we realise just how much of death there was in our lives and in church life. Repentance and brokenness were for us the place of a new approach, a new start. . . . There was no dramatic manifestation. My longing had been for another Pentecost—the visitation of the Spirit which I had read of in the revivals—but it was not so. For me personally, the first sign was a deep experience of peace and rest; I felt as if I had come home.[16]

It is wonderful when death is buried, but it cannot happen without conversion:

The church at Sardis needed to repent, to confess its deadness, to put away sin, to be filled with the Spirit, to put life and meaning into all these things they were doing. All of their work was but the striving of the flesh. They were not channels of the power of God.[17]

Many churches are in the same state. If your church is one of them, you might benefit from getting together with a small group for humble prayer, inviting the church leaders to participate, and letting in God's light on the situation from the pages of the Bible.

An obedient church

If the church wants to come back to life and freshness, it will need to put Christ at the very centre and to obey Him. Many will no doubt say, 'We would certainly like that, but haven't you noticed how small the group of believers is?' However, once we have gone through the list of things to consider and have decided to go ahead, we shall have to carry on with what we have and with the Lord: 'Nehemiah began with what he had. He didn't discard it, but sorted out the rubble from that which could be used.'[18]

I remember being in a similar situation quite a few years ago. The Belgian Evangelical Mission had asked me to take over one of their mission posts after my probationary year, and to build a church from it. We started with a handful of people. Some of them had a practical, active faith; others believed in Jesus Christ and the appropriate doctrines but did not see their way clear to active evangelism; they were doubtful whether it could still have effect today. After prayer, we formulated a dual plan. One part we called personal evangelism, the other mass evangelism. Our objective was to double the number of believers in three years. So we did have an objective, however modest it might have been. Personal evangelism began with the members of the group. They made up a list of prayer items and prayed for particular people. After a while, they would approach these people with a tract or copy of John's Gospel. Later on, they would invite them for an evening at their home. This way we were trying to do two things at once: to get everybody involved and teach them how to witness; and to try to win people for Jesus Christ.

Using mass evangelism we intended to reach the entire city with the message of the gospel. Our target was a population of over 60,000. That seemed impossible! So we decided to divide the city in parts and to get going all the same.

After one year of hard work there were still no results. Belgium was a difficult field of action, especially in those days. That was still before the Second Vatican Council and contact with Catholics was very difficult. We received grace from above to persevere and after a year or so a family was converted. This was the turning-point. These new converts breathed fresh air into the work. The others were encouraged by them. Another person was converted and yet another, and things got going little by little. As new life was injected into the group, expectations were raised. The vision increased as we reached our goals. We formulated a new goal and the Lord helped us towards it as well.

Today the church is still growing. We no longer are involved directly, but that is fine because it is not man's work. Jesus said, 'I will build my church, and the gates of Hades will not overcome it' (Mt 16:18). We need to have the right vision. Cuthbert points out that when God showed Ezekiel the valley of dry bones, He did not intend the prophet to rush down into the valley and try to put them together again:

Can you imagine the chaos if Ezekiel got it wrong—a man with odd legs and arms upside down! But he spoke the word, shared the vision, and the bones began to move. God is bringing people together. It needs men to prophesy, speak out the vision of God to every community. He will do the rest.[19]

When Christ again becomes the centre of all activity, things will go right. As the evangelist said, 'I talk about Christ at the beginning of my speech and at the end. In between I talk about Him as well.' So many things fall into place when we keep Him at the centre:

> Obedience to Christ thus was the very means by which those in His company learned more truth. He did not ask the disciples to follow what they did not know to be true, but no one could follow Him without learning what was true (John 7:17). Hence, Jesus did not urge His disciples to commit their lives to a doctrine, but to a Person Who was the doctrine and only as they continued in His word could they know the truth (John 8:31, 32).[20]

Churches may be revived if their basis is still sound and the embers are still glowing. A church, however, is a group of individuals; therefore, every one of us needs to search his own heart and ask himself, 'Could I be the ember that is needed to get the fire going again, so that once more it could be seen and produce warmth?'

Notes

[1] Michael Griffiths, 'Evangelism and Church Planting: Future Directions for Church Growth', in *How to Plant Churches*, pp 128–129.

[2] Bram Krol, *Onder Commando: een kompas voor de gemeente van Jezus Christus* (Telos Interlektur: Arnhem, 1979), p 155.

[3] *ibid*, p 156.

[4] *ibid*.

[5] D. C. Carp, *Wat geloven de 'evangelicals'?* (Amersfoort, 1980). Quoted in Bram Krol, *Gemeentegroei* (Buiten, Schipperheyn: Amsterdam, 1982), p. 82.

[6] Donald A. McGavran and Winfried C. Arn, *Ten Steps for Church Growth* (Harper & Row: San Francisco, 1977), p 25.

[7] *ibid*, p 27.

[8] *ibid*, p 28.

9   Eddie Gibbs, *Body Building Exercises for the Local Church* (Falcon: London, 1979), p 43.
10 Howard A. Snyder, *The Problem of Wineskins: Church Structure in a Technological Age* (Inter-Varsity Press: Downers Grove, Illinois, 1976), p 63.
11 Krol, *op cit,* p 102.
12 Vance Havner, *Messages on Revival* (Baker Book House: Grand Rapids, Michigan, 1986), p 62.
13 James F. Engel and Wilbert Norton, *What's Gone Wrong with the Harvest?* (Zondervan: Grand Rapids, Michigan, 1982), p 55.
14 Krol, *op cit,* p 71.
15 Andrew Kane, *Let There Be Life: The Pain and Joy of Renewal in a Local Church* (Falcon: London, 1979), pp 29–30.
16 ibid pp 31–32.
17 Havner, *op cit,* p 64.
18 Nick Cuthbert, *Rise Up and Build* (Kingsway Publications: Eastbourne, 1982), p 80.
19 *ibid,* p 60.
20 Robert E. Coleman, *The Master Plan of Evangelism* (Fleming H. Revell: Old Tappan, New Jersey, 1982), p 56.

PART II

4

Church Planting: It Can Be Done!

Givers and takers of God's grace—that is how you could describe Christians. To be a Christian is a gift and a task, a privilege and a reponsibility. We can depend on the promise of Jesus Christ, 'I will build my church', and the commission He gave us, 'Go and make disciples of all nations' (Mt 16:18; 28:19). How do we go about this task? Where and when do we start, and with whom? What if people are indifferent or perhaps even unwilling?

The Book of Proverbs says, 'He who wins souls is wise' (11:30). We need to act thoughtfully. People's situations differ greatly; often hearers are not keen to receive the good news of Jesus Christ. In Europe today most people are not particularly hungry for the gospel. But could we not whet their appetites? They are probably not interested because they have not yet tasted! Perhaps they have to see the good news in action before they want to hear about it. Eddie Gibbs has observed that 'In Church growth thinking the distinction is made between three kinds of evangelism. These are Presence Evangelism, Proclamation Evangelism and Persuasion Evangelism.'[1] For the sake of completeness we should add a fourth kind of evangelism: confrontation evangelism.

Presence evangelism

Most people around us do not know the gospel, or have a biased view of it. They are not aware of the state they are in and, consequently, what Jesus has accomplished has no value for them personally. I have met quite a few people who asked me, 'What good is there in believing? Why should I?'

The best way to capture their interest is just to be there with them, sharing our lives and the grace we have received from God. No proclamation, but service and sharing. No explanation, but our presence alone. After all, Jesus Christ started this way as well: 'The Word became flesh and lived for a while among us' (Jn 1:14). He entered this world and shared His life with us. He adapted completely to our sin-infected society. He shared in times of need, of pain, of sorrow and of joy. His presence preceded His message. John testifies later in his letter, 'That which was from the beginning, which we have heard, which we have seen with our eyes, which we have looked at and our hands have touched—this we proclaim concerning the Word of life' (1 Jn 1:1). God's good news was already visible and tangible before it was preached. We need to follow this example. All sorts of needs occupy people's minds. When we share their needs and concerns, we demonstrate the love of God. When they notice our sincere interest in them, they will open up to the beliefs which motivate us. Through us Christ wishes to show them who He is and what He wants to be to them.

Experienced missionaries distinguish two different needs in the lives of people. First and foremost is the need to know God. They themselves are often ignorant of this and are not conscious of their need. The second is commonly called 'a felt need.' Loneliness, disappointment, sadness or material needs—all of these are felt needs. People are conscious of them. When we are able to get close to people through their felt needs and to minister to them in that area, they might be more inclined to accept help for their actual needs. They are then able to see the love of Christ in action before they come to terms with the theory.

It is essential for us to be sincere in this approach. It is not a sales method: 'At the heart of the gospel preached and demonstrated by Jesus Christ were concern and compassion for man in every aspect of his life. . . . These things were not for purposes of propaganda; they represented instead a genuine expression of concern for others.'[2] But is gospel proclamation not part and parcel of this genuine concern? When our motives are pure, our main concerns are God's honour and our neighbour's well-being.

In living out the gospel we should not only think of those who live in desperate circumstances. We should be sensitive to the basic human need for love, hope, acceptance, respect, intimacy, understanding, a sense of belonging and harmony. As Christians we are in a position to be an example of God's love, concern, interest and grace by meeting those needs. This is how 'cold contacts' may be 'warmed up' for the sake of the gospel.

In Belgium, for example, postmen are allowed to deliver pensions and pay them right on your doorstep. I know of a Christian postman who always returns home late from his rounds. When somebody once asked him why he always finished late, he replied, 'I do not just deliver the mail; I have a parish to tend.' He is not cheating his employer; he is doing this in his free time. This man had built up such a ministry of love and care that he had grown to resemble Jesus Christ in his everyday life. This kind of evangelism has also been called 'friendship evangelism'. Its purpose is to instil in people who do not think they need the gospel an awareness that they do—to make people receptive to God's message.

Proclamation evangelism

One may, of course, do a lot of good works and not speak a word about Jesus. Sooner or later, people may ask if you are a vegetarian or something, because you are such a nice person. When this happens, we need to explain our relationship with God in a natural way for friendship evangelism to be effective. When we put it off for too long, it may be difficult to broach the subject at all. Once we received visitors in our home, the parents of a school friend of our youngest daughter Esther. After general conversation we discussed schools and the choices to be made for the future. We said in a casual way, 'We find it difficult at times to make the right choice. Yesterday evening we prayed for wisdom and understanding to keep us from making a mistake, since a lot depends on it.' The conversation continued naturally after this. The important thing was that we had witnessed about our relationship with God and about the way it has become an integral part of our lives. As Christians we do not live two lives at once—one spiritual and the other social. We therefore have the freedom to be ourselves and let our lives proclaim the gospel.

Presence evangelism raises questions in people's minds, and prepares them for the proclamation of God's message. Proclamation means explaining God's plan in straightforward language, as revealed in the Bible: where we come from, why we are in the situation we are in and where we are going. Sooner or later, we shall have to deal with the following questions:

1 God the Creator
2 The fact of sin
3 The punishment for sin
4 Christ took the punishment on Himself
5 Salvation is a gift
6 We need to accept it

We must ensure that we pass on the gospel in the right way. It is essential to bring out the relevance of the gospel to the person to whom we are speaking: 'The gospel communicator has the obligation to focus theological truth in such a way that it brings light upon each person's unique situation.'[3] This means that we need to proclaim that God cares for them and that they should learn to care about Him. The purpose of friendship evangelism is to acquaint people with the gospel and to make them ready to receive it. Proclamation is intended to lead people to a positive decision to give their lives to Jesus Christ. This is the stage where they receive information. They learn about the truth; there may not be a decision at this point. They need to understand the full scope of God's message before they can respond to it. I'd like to emphasise how important the witness of the ordinary Christian can be at this point. He or she has a power of conviction which surpasses by far that of the specialist, the minister or the missionary: 'There is no question that lay witness *generally* will be the most effective way to bring people to decision. It possesses high credibility and it obviously is the most personal of all media.'[4]

Proclamation evangelism can take place by organising a home Bible study, lending a book, giving an invitation to a meeting or through personal witnessing. God shows us all kinds of ways to pass on His message so that people hear and understand that God's word concerns them personally.

Persuasion evangelism

Simply informing our neighbour is not enough; he has to make a choice. The Bible spells this out for us very clearly. Back in Old Testament times Moses was ordered to proclaim, 'I have set before you life and death, blessings and curses. Now choose life, so that you and your children may live' (Deut 30:19). Israel had to be confronted with the fact that a choice was necessary. In the same way, the apostles and the early Christians set about convincing others. In Thessalonica, Paul and his team debated from Scripture, 'explaining and proving' what was God's plan, and 'Some of the Jews were persuaded' (Acts 17:3–4).

The same thing happened in Corinth: 'Every Sabbath he reasoned in the synagogue, trying to persuade Jews and Greeks' (Acts 18:4). At the end of Acts we read that Paul welcomed the Jewish leaders into his own rented house and 'From morning till evening he explained and declared to them the kingdom of God and tried to convince them about Jesus from the Law of Moses and from the Prophets' (Acts 28:23). Writing his second letter to the Corinthians, he explains his motives once more: 'Since, then, we know what it is to fear the Lord, we try to persuade men' (2 Cor 5:11).

In our zeal to win others we should do our utmost to convince them. There is nothing wrong about this. It has to be done. It is scriptural, and part of our responsibility: 'We cannot be responsible members of the Body unless we practice "intentional evangelism." Our *purpose* must be to win those who are living without the treasure.'[5]

This process has been beautifully expressed in John 17:7–8, in the high-priestly prayer of Jesus: 'Now they know that everything you have given me comes from you.' This is presence evangelism; the disciples had realised that it was from God. This leads on to proclamation evangelism: 'For I gave them the words you gave me. . .' The message was told and they heard the words of God. Finally, there is persuasion evangelism: '. . . and they accepted them. They knew with certainty that I came from you, and they believed that you sent me.' The disciples were convinced, accepted the message and then found the salvation that is in Christ.

Therefore, when the time is ripe, we must compel our friends to take a firm stand. We have to make them understand that no decision is really a decision. When you do not accept an offer, you have in fact turned it down. The Bible is very plain about this: we are lost if we leave things as they are: 'Whoever believes in the Son has eternal life, but whoever rejects the Son will not see life, for God's wrath remains on him' (Jn 3:36). The gospel is God's offer to save those who are lost. When they do not take the hand stretched out to them, they will remain in their lost state and will ultimately be judged. The grey, neutral zone which we often prefer to stay in, does not in fact exist. You are either for something or against something; you walk either in darkness or in the light. The purpose of this stage in evangelism is obvious: people need to come to a decision.

Confrontation evangelism

There will be times when we shall have to insist that people make a choice. This is not very pleasant, either for them or for us. Most often this situation arises with people who know the truth but do not want to be converted. They have seen and understood, they know what they have to do, but refuse to take that step. They are like the people of Israel whom God called stiff-necked and hard-hearted. God sent his prophets in a last attempt to call his people back. The prophets forced upon them the truth which they knew but did not want to obey, 'because they were stiff-necked and would not listen to my words' (Jer 19:15). Then God proclaimed what would befall them if they did not change their ways. Judgement would come on them. Clearly, this method of proclamation was not the first God had tried. It was, in effect, a last resort in order to make them understand that they were to awaken from the intoxication of sin and momentary pleasure and turn to God again.

At times, a drastic measure like this was necessary, as church history and the New Testament show. Luther, for example, made use of this method in his attempt to restore the Catholic Church and to make her obedient to God's word. In the Acts of the Apostles we find Paul involved several times in confrontation evangelism. Paul debated with Jews in the synagogues, proving from the Scriptures which they all knew that Jesus of Nazareth was God's Anointed, the Messiah.

In Corinth, for example, Paul first talked in the synagogue; this started regular debates which developed into a confrontation. Scripture says that 'But when the Jews opposed Paul and became abusive, he shook out his clothes in protest and said to them, "Your blood be on your own heads! I am clear of my responsibility. From now on I will go to the Gentiles"' (Acts 18:6). The miraculous thing, however, is that the person living next door to the synagogue was converted, as well as Crispus, the synagogue ruler, together with his entire household. There was confrontation in Ephesus, and again in Jerusalem, when Paul had to appear before Felix, 'who was well acquainted with the Way'. Felix came with his wife Drusilla and sent for Paul. The apostle then unequivocally put before them the choice, since they had been informed but did not want to act accordingly: 'As Paul discoursed on righteousness, self-control and the judgment to come, Felix was afraid' (Acts 24:22, 24–25).

Therefore, when the situation requires it, we should not shrink from proclaiming the gospel in this way. Whether or not people will go on liking us afterwards is not an issue. In the final account, we should be concerned not with ourselves, but with the honour of God and the salvation of everyone we meet. When a bridge over the highway has collapsed and you position yourself half a mile from the disaster area with a red flag, people can be expected to grumble about it. Why are you holding me up? Why do you not let me drive on?

This is the case with confrontation evangelism. As we know from the word of God what will befall us if we do not turn to God for forgiveness, we are called to present people with the choice in a spirit of love. You might follow the example of the man who took his friend by the shoulders, gave him a good shaking, looked him straight in the eyes and said, 'I am more concerned about your eternal destination than you yourself are.' First, however, this man had wrestled in prayer for his friend's salvation. Take care you do the same! We could, perhaps, illustrate the process with the following diagram:

Our job >	Presence >	Proclamation >	Persuasion >		Confrontation
People's condition /	unaware and ignorant of the gospel	aware of the gospel	understanding personal consequences	C O N V E R S I O N	refusal to accept the gospel
Our action	show love	explain God's word	apply God's word		show the consequences
Our purpose /	prepare for proclamation	prepare them to decide	prompt them towards a decision		final attempt to prompt towards a positive decision

Overcoming apathy

Some people are not open to the gospel. They hide behind an armour of indifference as soon as spiritual matters are touched upon. Although we should keep in mind that the Holy Spirit alone can open hearts, it is for us to find the best approach possible: 'God's Spirit is not limited, people are. We can blunder terribly in the approach we choose. For the listener this appproach is their point of contact with the gospel. The way we go about it then becomes the determining factor.'[6] We must beware of hiding behind the truth that the Spirit accomplishes everything. This is true enough, but let us not forget that the Spirit resides in us. He wants to be active through us. He is the Spirit of creation and enables us to be creative in the way we approach people with His message. McGavran underlines the importance of this when he says that 'In great measure, responsiveness is related to approach.'[7]

In the Belgian Evangelical Mission we have thought very carefully about this problem of indifference. Certain contacts and friends, to whom we started to talk about the gospel, responsed politely, 'We like you as a person, but we are not really interested in God.' So what do you do? How do you conquer indifference?

A key

One day, when we were thinking and praying seriously about this problem at one of our mission posts, we were given a new understanding: when there is a casual relationship, but no interest in God and His word, a good response would be: 'It is rather unwise not to be interested in something you know little about.' This could work as a challenge because everyone likes the next person to think that he or she is wise. Explain then that you are convinced that their lack of interest is caused by ignorance. Tell them that the picture they have formed on the basis of what they know is probably inaccurate. Therefore, they are deluded into thinking that they know when they do not really know at all.

You could invite them for an open and honest conversation and say, 'There might be things you can teach me about life. On the other hand, I am convinced I have some information that you either don't have or have only partly, and probably incorrectly. By talking about it, we can help each other. You are free to believe or disbelieve what I am going to say, but you can only make a judgement when you have the information. You won't lose anything by spending a few evenings with me and exchanging views. When you know the facts, you can then decide whether you are interested or not. No need to worry that I'll pursue you for ever. If you decide, having taken everything in, that you do not want any of it, I shall respect that.'

The person in charge of the mission post set to work on this basis. He said to himself, 'We might have found a key to open doors which have been closed to us so far. When I meet with a positive response, I should be well prepared.' He put together a series of five studies which we have called 'the five evenings'. His notes contain a statement of purpose, a subject outline for each evening, a list of standard answers and standard objections, and a short bibliography. It is for preparation purposes only and is not taken on our visits. 'The five evenings' deal with the following basic topics.

1 The word of God

God reveals Himself to us. How did the Bible come to us? How do we know it can be trusted? We discuss the external as well as internal evidence for the reliability of the Scriptures. How did Jesus use the Scriptures? He puts us under its authority in John 12. What matters here is that a change of authority takes place in the minds of those we reason with. They should come to accept that it is the only reliable foundation upon which to build their lives (Mt 7).

2 Creator and creation

When this topic is announced for the following week, most people protest, 'We believe in evolution.' They appreciate the fact that we have brought up the topic because they sense that we are willing to discuss openly a position which they think is difficult to maintain. Usually we have a lively discussion on the second evening! We should be able, quite naturally, to refute the evolution argument without showing arrogance. It is not necessary to win the discussion but to show how shaky evolutionist arguments really are and how much 'faith' is needed to uphold them. After a couple of hours we usually suggest that we stop the argument and read the first few chapters of the Bible. Most people have never read them in their entirety.

Having read a passage we take time to explain it. We do not go into all the details, but just follow the logic of it. Then people begin to see the magnificence of man in the beginning, when he was appointed to oversee creation. Modern humanism cannot match this. We read on to Genesis chapter 3, the origin of all troubles. We humans were the ones who opened the door to problems. Decay came in as a result. This is where the problem of nuclear arms started, of AIDS, apartheid, world hunger, war and family quarrels, and all the rest. It is as modern as today's newspaper. When we explain things this way we answer the question that everybody asks: 'How is it possible that there is a God of love, who is all powerful and yet allows such a lot of suffering in this world?' This second evening is not easy, but the knife of truth will cut deep.

3 The person of Jesus Christ

This is the subject for the third evening. The emphasis is on the fact that Jesus is God and is risen from the dead. We find ourselves in the field of apologetics, defending our faith. This should not alarm us. Our aim is to show that it is more logical to believe that Jesus Christ rose from the dead than to believe that his body was stolen or lost.

Luke's gospel starts with a declaration of dependability. Just read the first four verses. In the Acts of the Apostles Luke makes use of eyewitness accounts of Jesus' resurrection. The apostles testified powerfully about this event and they were willing to give their lives for it. We now come face to face with the Person of Jesus. He provides the answer to our problems, and challenges our preconceived ideas.

4 Mankind

This subject also meets with instant approval. After all, we live in a man-oriented society. Our main concern is to explain by way of the 'bridge illustration' where we are, who we are and where we are heading. The appendix gives details of this method of gospel proclamation.

What needs to be emphasised here is our inability to achieve our own salvation. When we explain in the right way, we shall almost certainly be asked at the end, 'How do I get to the other side? How can I make sure that things will turn out all right for me?' Our answer to this is, 'We shall tell you next time.' Experience has taught us that you should not give a reply right there and then. Most often the reaction is an emotional one, made on the spur of the moment when people begin to sense their lost state. The Holy Spirit, however, will 'convict the world of guilt in regard to sin and righteousness and judgment' (Jn 16:8). It is He who needs to convince our listeners. An immediate answer would reach no deeper than the emotions of the moment. Instead, we leave people in their lost state and let them be conscious of it. During that week we pray fervently that the Holy Spirit will convince them. Normally we draw the bridge illustration on a piece of paper and leave it behind, reminding our contacts that something is missing in their lives.

5 Salvation

This is the final subject in the series. Here we pick up where we left off on the fourth evening, repeat briefly what we discussed earlier and raise the final question. Then we let the Bible explain that we cannot come to God but that in His eternal goodness He came down to us in Christ. We show what Christ has accomplished for us and how His sacrifice for our sins bridges the gap and clears the way for a restored relationship with God. He invites us to come. He calls us to accept His salvation.

In this approach we use four evenings for building a solid foundation. The Bible is discussed first, then the authority of the Creator, and then Jesus Christ. From this perspective man will come to see who he is and why he needs to obey God's calling.

Open doors

The enjoyable thing brought about by discovering this method was seeing new faces when I returned six months later to preach. I met new people after the service and asked whether they had been Christians for a long time. No, they had not. How did you become Christians, I then asked, and was told their story: 'We liked the evangelist, but were not interested in God or the Bible. He asked us if he could explain the gospel, because he was convinced we had not understood it properly and for that reason were not interested. We ended up spending five evenings talking together and finally realised we certainly had not understood it, so we came here.'

What a joy! This appproach has been followed on a large scale and, although it might not always be successful, we believe that we have found a key. In the process we have seen many people being converted.

Notes

[1]   Eddie Gibbs, *I Believe in Church Growth* (Hodder & Stoughton: London, 1985), p 147.

[2]   R. Kenneth Strachan, *The Inescapable Calling* (William B. Eerdmans: Grand Rapids, Michigan, 1968), pp 73–74.

[3]   James F. Engel and Wilbert Norton, *What's Gone Wrong with the Harvest*? (Zondervan: Grand Rapids, Michigan, 1982), p 68.

[4]   *ibid*, p 98.

[5]   Donald A. McGavran and Winfield C. Arn, *Ten Steps for Church Growth* (Harper & Row; San Francisco, 1977), p 55.

[6]   Leen La Riviere, 'Succesvol evangeliseren', in *Evangelisatie*, ed Leen La Riviere (J.H. Kok: Kampen, 1980), p 18.

[7]   McGavran and Arn, *op cit*, p 76.

5

Church Planting: Spiritual Warfare

In Europe we have arrived at the post-Christian era. Some people call it the pre-Christian era. Either way, we need to acknowledge that Europe at the moment consists of cultivated pagans. People first need to have something to believe in before we can call them to believe. Gospel proclamation done in this way is a form of teaching. It is interesting to see that Paul calls himself 'a herald and an apostle' in the first letter to Timothy, but then goes on to describe himself as a 'teacher of the true faith to the Gentiles' (1 Tim 2:7). He was a messenger to the Jews and a teacher to the Gentiles. In *Evangelism and the Sovereignty of God*, J. I. Packer says about Paul's ministry, 'His primary task in evangelism was to teach the truth about the Lord Jesus Christ.' [1] He goes on to discuss the content of this teaching and includes the following points:

1 God—His existence and His nature
2 Sin—our falling short of God's standard
3 Jesus Christ—His Person and saving work
4 The need for faith and repentance in obedience to the Lord.[2]

This sort of teaching is still needed today. In his course on evangelism, I. J. Fontenot writes, 'a person must have a proper knowledge of the truth before he can volitionally believe!'[3] He goes on to explain how the theologians of Jesus' day had taken away the key to knowledge (Mk 7:1–23; Lk 11:52) by their traditions which kept both themselves and others from entering. It is the task of the person who is witnessing to bring back the key to knowledge by Bible teaching, that is to say, by comparing scripture with scripture (Mal 2:7). This is how evangelism should be done in Europe today–by teaching.

Opposition

There will always be people who oppose the gospel. This can be utterly frustrating. Dee Brestin writes, 'I can think of three ways to challenge, to soften, apathetic hearts. . . .
1   Pray
2   Persist in loving them into the kingdom
3   Provoke their thoughts with questions and the word.'[4]

We are bound to meet people whom we shall never win. In the final account, this is God's business, not ours. Nevertheless, I am encouraged by a story about an evangelist from Austria. He was deeply distressed and at the end of his tether. During a day of fasting and prayer he cried out to God, 'Why isn't there a single soul who wants to hear about you?' God replied, 'Why ask *me*? Ask *them*!' He did precisely that. He made a list of five questions. The first question asked, 'I have come to the conclusion that people no longer wish to hear about God. Could you tell me why?' The last was, 'If you had the opportunity to talk openly about life, together with some others in a home, would you be interested?' He went from door to door for a while with his questionnaire at a time of the day when both husband and wife were at home. And what was the result? In a few days he had made appointments for six home Bible studies with eight to ten people attending. In the face of opposition he prayed, listened to God's voice and obeyed. We need to do the same.

Social relationships

We are only able to live up to the challenge to be the salt and light of this world when we are exposed to decay and darkness. We are not of the world, but we are in the world. The call to live holy lives and abandon worldly pleasures can have unfortunate results; some Christians only have contact with other Christians, apart from in their professional occupations. This was not Jesus' way, and it becomes difficult to win people from the world when our contacts with them are superficial. Only by living in this world and being different will we gain recognition, and people will come to notice that God's Spirit lives in us. This is of paramount importance if gospel proclamation is to be effective.

Peter Wagner maintains that about one tenth of all Christians might have the gift of evangelism, though not all make use of their gift. He argues that 'only a certain number of Christians have the *gift of evangelist*, but every Christian has the *role of witness*. These two . . . must combine to mobilize the maximum force for evangelism in your church.'[5] He goes on to explain that new Christians–recent converts–are most effective in winning others for Christ. Our own experience confirms this. The fire of first love is catching!

Young Christians are so full of what they have found in Christ that they cannot help speaking about it. There are two more reasons for their effectiveness in winning others. They have not yet acquired our evangelical jargon, so they are able to express themselves in a way that non-Christians understand. Second, they are in contact with those who still need to be won for Christ. According to Wagner, 'The effectiveness of the Christian's role as a witness for church growth decreases with that person's maturity in Christ.'[6] He estimates that within two or three years all their friends are Christians, either because their non-Christian friends have accepted Christ, or because they are no longer in contact with them.[7]

In the light of this fact, we should help young Christians to win others at the stage when their witness is especially effective. Older Christians need to examine their lives. Why is it that we no longer have contact with non-Christians? Dee

Brestin shows how we can win others for Christ. She entitles her book *Finders Keepers* and explains her choice of title as follows: 'Finding: Making friends with non-Christians and loving them into the kingdom; Keeping: Teaching those who seem to believe to obey all that Jesus commanded.'[8] She then shares her conviction, gained after interviewing many Christians, that something is not right. A list of reasons is given why Christians have no time to develop relationships with non-Christians.

Materialism is one of them. We are busy acquiring riches instead of finding people for the kingdom of Heaven. Meeting mania is another. We are so busy being active in our local church, and going from worship service to church meeting, and from prayer meeting to Bible study that we have no time for the sheep that are lost.

We need to learn all over again how to make social contacts. In the Belgian Evangelical Mission we decided that the members of our year teams should join a social or sports club. In this way they integrate themselves into the life of the city where they have just moved to and develop relationships there. They are then in a position to invite people for a cup of coffee, and find they are invited back by their new friends. This has proved to be very effective because it allows them to tell people about God's love in a non-aggressive way and to show the importance of it in their own lives from day to day.

When someone is converted, an entire family or circle of friends opens up, and we have seen many come to faith in this way. Bram Krol speaks of a 'web movement' in this respect, 'a stage in between a corporate and a personal conversion.'[9] We need to pray that God's message 'may spread rapidly and be honoured' (2 Thess 3:1). Making use of our social contacts could well be part of the answer to our prayers.

The decisive action of God

Our risen Lord promised His disciples power, *dunamis*, to be

His witnesses (Acts 1:8). When we take a close look at the apostles and their followers, we see how the Lord lives up to His promise. The particular means God uses are:

1 The word of God
2 The Spirit of God
3 The man who serves God.

Of course, it would be more accurate to say, 'the person who serves God'. Women and men are equally useful in God's hands, though they may have different functions.

These three means nearly always operate together. God's Spirit works through a person, granting power to their testimony. Scripture is used by this person under the guidance of the Spirit. So it is important to take these three elements into account in our desire to win others. We shall, therefore, discuss them in detail.

The word of God

A while ago, I had contact with a man who liked to talk about spiritual things but would not apply them to his personal life. We had some interesting conversations, during which I attempted to give Scripture-based answers to his questions. My aim was to let the Bible speak, rather than speaking myself. He tired of it after a while and asked, 'Why do you always drag in that dead book? I want to hear what *you* have to say. We are alive today and that Bible is nearly 2,000 years old. We should write another one for this day and age. Why don't you throw it away?' We continued our conversation and soon I had to answer another one of his questions. I opened my Bible, read a few verses and explained it to him. You can imagine his reaction! But I continued using the Bible and explained why I did so. That man was converted.

A few weeks later I asked him, 'Jeff, what exactly made you decide to be converted?' He replied, 'I was convinced by the Bible in which I had no faith at first.' This was one of the first lessons he learned and he went on to communicate it to others.

There is no need for us to be anxious when people make scornful remarks about the Bible. When threatened with a knife, you could say, 'I am not afraid, it is a stage prop, it is just rubber.' What does the other person have to do to convince you it is real? He simply has to use it!

So it is with the Bible. Sometimes we need to defend the Bible against attacks, but at all times we need to keep using it. God Himself says that His word is living and powerful and 'Sharper than any double-edged sword, it penetrates even to dividing soul and spirit, joints and marrow; it judges the thoughts and attitudes of the heart' (Heb 4:12). We should not be side-tracked by criticism of the Bible and let God's weapon be taken away from us, 'the sword of the Spirit, which is the word of God' (Eph 6:17). It achieves what human words cannot do: 'Begin with the audience and focus the Word of God on people so that it speaks to their needs.'[10]

This is how the apostles went about their ministry and it granted authority to their words. We are not apostles in the same sense as the first twelve were, but we are just as much 'sent out' into this world as they were, to pass on the good news in God's name. We are ambassadors and therefore need to transmit the word of the One who sent us. According to J. I. Packer, if the gospel is to advance we need to 'be taught afresh to testify to our Lord and to His gospel, in public and in private, in preaching and in personal dealing, with boldness, patience, power, authority and love.'[11]

The Spirit of God

In the Acts of the Apostles Luke mentions that the apostles witnessed again and again, filled with the Holy Spirit. Chapter 2 shows them at Pentecost. Chapter 4 shows them in front of the elders and Pharisees, and later on in one of their prayer meetings. In Chapter 7 'Stephen, full of the Holy Spirit, looked up to heaven and saw the glory of God and . . . the Son of Man standing at the right hand of God' (Acts 7:55). In chapter 11 we see Barnabas at work, 'a good man, full of the Holy Spirit and faith' (Acts 11:24).

Jesus Christ fulfilled His promise and sent the Spirit to all who put their trust in Him by faith. It is clear that the power of their testimony was the power of the Holy Spirit. This remains true today. He alone is able to convince people of sin and of their need for a Saviour. Jesus said, 'When he comes, he will convict the world of guilt in regard to sin and righteousness and judgment: in regard to sin, because men do not believe in me' (Jn 16:8–9).

Have you ever tried to convince someone that swearing or stealing is sinful? Just try it and you will see how quickly people defend what they are doing. 'After all, others do it too.' 'It is just a habit.' 'I don't really mean what I said.' However, when you set about convincing someone that not believing in Jesus is a sin too, then you are in for trouble. People get indignant: 'I can believe what I like! God cannot force me to believe. He can ask me if I want to believe, but no more than that. I cannot accept that not believing is sinful.'

The power of the Holy Spirit has to convince us that it is sinful not to believe in Jesus of Nazareth. A wonderful thing then happens. All other sins are recognised as sin as well! Only when we step into the light are we able to see how we are covered in filth. In order to touch people's hearts and make them see that they are in need of God's grace and forgiveness, we need to speak the right words at the right time.

How can we witness through God's Spirit working in us? First, we need to acknowledge the sovereignty of God: 'The wind blows wherever it pleases' (Jn 3:8). It is hardly surprising that this statement is part of the chapter which deals with being born again. Scripture tells us that we have the responsibility to allow God to fill us with the Holy Spirit. When we heed His warnings and live by faith, God will keep His promise and fill us time and again. At the same time we need to be guided by faith when we meet people. We need to try to understand them. God's Spirit will lead us, as He promised, if we are available for Him at all times. Prayer is an important element in conjunction with witnessing. We can water the planted seed with prayer.

So we have to act in obedience to Jesus, just like the servants did at the wedding at Cana. When Jesus told them to 'draw some out and take it to the master of the banquet' (Jn 2:8), He asked them to act in faith. They drew water but tasted wine. While they carried out orders, the Lord acted in power. The proclamation of the gospel follows the same pattern. What we tell people is mere words, and what we give them to read is no more than paper and ink. But in some miraculous way, the Spirit of God changes this into the life-renewing knowledge of Jesus Christ. Take this into account and put your trust in it. When blessings come, you will find it easy to give the honour to God.

The man who serves God

God could have written the message of John 3:16 in bold letters of fire across the heavens but He chose not to. He could have sent down angels to make known His message to all nations, but instead He allows people who partake of His salvation to be His heralds. We are 'a chosen people, a royal priesthood, a holy nation, a people belonging to God, that [we] may declare the praises of him who called [us] out of darkness into his wonderful light' (1 Pet 2:9). This is the essence of witnessing. You need to experience salvation before you can talk about it. It is not just a matter of words. It involves all of our life. The Christian is an example of what God is willing to do in people's lives: 'The gospel is not merely truth; it is a way and it is a life.'[12] It is of vital importance, therefore, that we let Christ be Lord of our life. This is a formidable challenge:

If the Christian church is to make an impact upon the world

today, then in faithfulness to God's Word, with disregard of all risks and acceptance of all consequences, it must return to a witness that is characterized by obedience in the verbal proclamation of the gospel, in consistent demonstration of its life, in disinterested service to others, and in the sacrificial spirit that has taken the cross to heart.[13]

In this way the Lord wants to use us in order to make us resemble Christ and pass on His word by living it out.

God makes himself known

Something needs to be added to all of this. The gospel is not just another ideology for us to embrace. It is not a choice from a range of equal possibilities. God is the living God. He is the eternal self-sufficient God, infinite and exalted. This God has spoken to us and revealed Himself, and He makes Himself heard today:

> It is important that the supernatural quality of the gospel be introduced to people. The message of Christ is not just a moral code or a philosophy of life. The gospel gives us access to a Person who died and rose again. The gospel offers exciting scenes of divine intervention in the lives of ordinary people. This most often shows in the first instance in their conversion.[14]

We cannot overlook the supernatural, even though it might be a subject of debate. In this area that we feel our inadequacy and smallness, but that is no reason for hiding our heads in the sand, or declaring that God no longer intervenes miraculously as He did in the old days.

John Wimber has described how straight after his conversion he formed a picture of the ideal local church. He expected great things to happen: 'It was a vision taken from the book of Acts. What I soon discovered was that most Christians do not come together to prepare for battle with Satan and conquer territory for Jesus Christ.'[15] It is a fact that few

Christians expect God to make Himself known when they talk about Him. Western Christians tend to accommodate themselves to a rationalistic gospel that makes sense intellectually. But where is the power in this?: 'What Christians–including evangelicals–are often left to follow is a good moral example, not a dynamic, Satan-conquering faith in the Lord.'[16]

We need to be vigilant lest we fall into extremes. We cannot work miracles. It is not for us to show off with manifestations of God's power. He is sovereign. We need to learn how to pray according to the will of God at all times, including times of difficulty and utter complexity. We then trust in God and expect Him to act.

Peter Wagner observes that 'Prayer has been preached, taught, sung about, and generally extolled in every church I have been connected with.'[17] But he goes on to question what kind of power we pray for. Are we expecting the manifestation of God's glory through our lives? A Christian with a strong witnessing ministry once told me, 'Sometimes you get stuck in a situation where you are trying to win people for Christ. Then God makes things happen so that it is necessary for Him to intervene. You need to pray in faith and then God will convince these people that He lives and cares for us all.'

To maintain that God's miraculous action is a thing of the past is equal to rewriting the Bible. If you handle the Scriptures fairly, it is extremely difficult to defend the argument that God's wondrous deeds stop where the New Testament canon stops. God has not changed. Like the apostles, we are confronted with an enormous task when we look at the billions of people we still have to reach with the gospel:

> If signs and wonders were an essential part of the ministry of the Lord and of his disciples, and if they are inseparably linked to the commission to preach the gospel, the conclusion is unavoidable that they may and should have a place in Christian mission for as long as the Great Commission is in force.[18]

We do not need to go around hunting for miracles, but we do need to be on the offensive against the realm of darkness. If we are, we then find that the Lord brings us into situations where it matters who is stronger!

It is normal for people to be fascinated by the supernatural. In *It's Friday, but Sunday's Comin'*, Anthony Campolo quotes the Russian novelist Fyodor Dostoyevsky:

> Man seeks not so much God as the miraculous. And as man cannot bear to be without miracles, he will create new miracles of his own for himself, and will worship deeds of sorcery and witchcraft, though he might be a hundred times over a rebel, heretic and infidel.[19]

Further on, Campolo tells about his experience at a university, when a woman came up to him with a crippled child whose legs were in calipers. The woman told him that God had sent him to heal her child. Somewhat embarrassed, Campolo retired to a backroom, together with the college chaplain, anointed the child's head with oil, laid hands on him and prayed for healing.

God revealed Himself in a sudden and amazing way. They were struck with awe and fear, God's presence was so powerful. A miraculous healing would not have surprised them. This, however, did not happen. Three years later the woman came up to Campolo again in a worship service and declared her child had been healed completely. She described how the next morning he woke up crying and she loosened the calipers a little. The same thing happened again the next morning, and the next, until the child's legs were completely straight.[20]

God likes to surprise us and we should never rule out the unexpected. But it would be untruthful to preach that God heals everyone every time. The Bible does not teach that, nor does experience. On the other hand, it is just as inaccurate to rule out His supernatural activity. We can expect God to go with us and lead the way, especially when evangelism leads us into conflict with the powers of darkness.

In home Bible studies with people who are eager to receive the word, I usually ask if I could say a prayer. They often welcome the idea. Then I ask each of them what I should pray for. That question might prove slightly embarrassing since most people do not expect it and are puzzled by it. Most expect me to pray an 'Ave Maria' or the Lord's Prayer. I then explain that I have a special relationship with God and am free to call Him Father! So I can request things of Him. After a moment's silence a few prayer requests are suggested. Then I begin to say a short prayer, straight from the heart, and expect God to do the rest. More often than not everyone will be quiet for a while when the prayer is over. Sometimes there are tears in their eyes, because no one has ever prayed for them personally before. One week later, when we meet again, I ask for news of someone we prayed for. At this point people exclaim in disbelief, 'Do you really believe that things might have changed because you prayed?' My stock answer is, 'No, not because I prayed for it, but because God hears you, loves you and is able.'

Do you recognise what is happening here? There has been an expression of confidence in the God of the supernatural. Not by way of a stage spectacle, but in all simplicity and dependency on God so we can minister to our fellow men in His name and make known who He is. Jesus is risen and is active among us.

It goes without saying that this leaves us vulnerable. What if God does *not* answer our prayers? We are in the midst of battle and depend on God for everything, leaving the final outcome to Him. What a challenge that is!

Notes

[1] J. I. Packer, *Evangelism and the Sovereignty of God* (Inter-Varsity Press: Downers Grove, Illinois, 1961), p 46.
[2] *ibid*, pp 58–71.

[3] I. J. Fontenot, 'A Two Hour Bible Course on Evangelism', Thesis, Dallas Theological Seminary, pp 2/20.

[4] Dee Brestin, *Finders Keepers* (Hodder & Stoughton: London, 1984), pp 132–133.

[5] C. Peter Wagner, *Your Church Can Grow: Seven Vital Signs of a Healthy Church* (Regal Books: Ventura, California, 1984), p 85.

[6] *ibid*, p 91.

[7] *ibid*, p 92.

[8] Brestin, *op cit*, p 11.

[9] Bram Krol, *Gemeentegroei* (Buiten, Schipperheyn: Amsterdam, 1982), p 41.

[10] James F. Engel and Wilbert Norton, *What's Gone Wrong with the Harvest?* (Zondervan: Grand Rapids, Michigan, 1982), p 42.

[11] Packer, *op cit*, p 125.

[12] R. Kenneth Strachan, *The Inescapable Calling* (William B. Eerdmans: Grand Rapids, Michigan, 1968), p 72.

[13] *ibid*, p 75.

[14] Melvin L. Hodges, *Un guide pour l'implantation d'églises* (Les Assemblées de Dieu: Brussels, 1977), p 24.

[15] John Wimber, *Power Evangelism: Signs and Wonders Today* (Hodder & Stoughton: London, 1985), p 13.

[16] *ibid*, p 108.

[17] C. Peter Wagner, *On the Crest of the Wave: Becoming a World Christian* (Regal Books: Ventura, California, 1983), pp 123–124.

[18] Strachan, *op cit*, p 62.

[19] Fyodor Dostoyevsky, *The Brothers Karamazov*, 'The Grand Inquisitor'. Quoted in Anthony Campolo, *It's Friday, But Sunday's Comin'* (Word Books: Waco, Texas, 1984), p 74.

[20] *ibid*, pp 75–80.

6

Church Planting: The Practical Approach

A couple came to me a few years ago and asked, 'Could we not plant a church in our region?' Faced with questions like this we need to be careful. Is the initiative inspired by concern for man in his lost state, or are there other motives? In this case, after much prayer and consideration, we came to the conclusion that their motives were God-given.

Soon we faced the question we considered in Chapter 2: Where do you start? We decided to look for people who were ready to receive the gospel. But how do you find them? We need to be open to the leading of God's Spirit and pray daily for encounters prepared by God. Bill Bright has called these 'divine appointments'.

This is a part of church planting but we need a more general plan of action. I would like to discuss five possible plans in this chapter, but of course the list is not exhaustive. God is able to provide us with creative ideas, allowing us to force our way into enemy territory and plant His church there. We stand firm on His promise that 'I will build my church, and the gates of Hades will not overcome it' (Mt 16:18). What strikes us in this promise of Christ is that where He builds, the powers from the realm of our foe will not be able to hinder.

The evangelistic campaign

For many people this heading immediately conjures up Billy Graham and his team. That, however, is not what we have in mind. In the first place, that type of campaign is on too large a scale, and unsuitable for a small group. Second, our campaign aims to mobilise local Christians to do the work of evangelism. However, it is interesting to see that a new kind of evangelism has emerged which differs from campaigns using visiting evangelists. This has been dubbed 'saturation evangelism'. Kenneth Strachan, who started this form of evangelism in Latin America, called it 'evangelism in depth'.[1] The emphasis was on involving local believers in a nationwide effort. Again, this is far too extensive for what we have in mind with church planting. An evangelistic campaign in the framework of the BEM is confined to a particular area. It is more manageable, much cheaper and can be organised by a relatively small group.

The activities have a local flavour because they are adapted to the inhabitants of a particular city. All kinds of variations can be introduced to make the approach as personal as possible. The size of the campaign team varies from twenty to fifty participants. We recruit our team members from nearby towns or even from neighbouring countries. When a team takes on an international or interdenominational character, it is helpful because the appearance of a sect is avoided. The campaign continues for a period of two or three weeks. Activities include drama and singing in the streets, giving out invitations to films or meetings, door-to-door evangelism with questionnaires and special activities for children and teenagers. The BEM has two canal barges, used to invite people to come on board and see our programme. Our 'gospel truck' has a video programme and several other attractions.

A campaign achieves several things at once. First, our team provides a united testimony to the peace and joy we experience as Christians. A programme of singing, music, and short testimonies often touches people's hearts. Following this we give away leaflets. Third, and most importantly, we are able to discover those who are willing to exchange views about the gospel. Often we see people who have been prepared by

God's Spirit accept Jesus in a campaign like this.

Others are willing to discuss the gospel, but are not ready to join anything. There is no need to hurry; we make an appointment to meet when the campaign is over, to talk about the Bible together. Many home Bible studies have started in this way, and such a start could lead to planting a church. It might also benefit an existing church when its evangelistic contacts have dried up.

It is of the utmost importance that follow-up should be well organised. To make people hungry for the gospel and then fail to feed them afterwards is unethical. So there needs to be a leader who is able to minister to all those interested during and right after the campaign. A campaign like this is a blessing to the believers who take part in it. They are greatly encouraged in their faith. Because they participate in work that challenges faith, they go beyond the limits of their own resources. Try it for yourself!

A church planting team

A powerful force is at work when we function as a team in proclaiming the gospel. Ever since 1972 the BEM has worked with 'church planting training teams' in Belgium. The experience has taught us the importance of Jesus' teaching about harmony (Mt 18:19–20), mutual love (Jn 13:35) and respect (Jn 17:20–23). The name of these teams indicates their purpose: to train people and to build a church. When team activity is not done in the right way, the damage can be worse than when one person is in charge. A number of people are involved and that means a higher risk. There has to be thorough planning. This strategy has given rise to several churches in Belgium, proof of the positive effects of working with teams.

An important principle comes into operation when we work together as a team to plant a church. The presence of Jesus among us is a vivid reality. Jesus said, 'Again, I tell you that if two of you on earth agree about anything you ask for, it will be done for you by my Father in heaven. For where two or three come together in my name, there I am with them' (Mt 18:19–20). God has promised to be with us always: 'Never will I leave you; never will I forsake you' (Heb 13:5). When we are alone in the woods or walking along the shore, He is there with us. But when we are together in His name, He is among us—He is present in a special way.

Being 'united in His name' means that I do not insist on getting my own way. What matters is that, united in Christ, we deny ourselves and let His will be done. This is what it means to 'agree about anything you ask for'. He is our Lord in a very practical way, and when this spirit reigns supreme among us, then *He* is among us. That is a wonderful thing, and the world around us will notice it. We cannot fake it, however. It needs to be real, it needs to be from God.

On two separate occasions in John's Gospel the Lord told us how the world would know by our behaviour that we were disciples of His. The first is in John 13:35: 'All men will know that you are my disciples if you love one another.' This is the essential condition: to love with the same love He had for us, the *agape* or selfless love. The Lord intends to pour out this love in us by the indwelling of the Holy Spirit. When we love others in the Christian family, everyone will know that we are His disciples. His presence is manifested among us in a way that is not possible for an individual Christian. It needs to come from God, but it can only truly function when we are a group.

Jesus spoke on this subject again in John 17:20–21, in his high-priestly prayer: 'My prayer is not for them alone. I pray also for those who will believe in me through their message, that all of them may be one, Father, just as you are in me and I am in you. May they also be in us so that the world may believe that you have sent me.' The unity among Christians that Jesus spoke of helps the world to recognise that Jesus Christ is the One whom the Father sent.

As can be expected, this verse is often quoted with reference to world-wide unity of all Christians. We need to concern ourselves with local unity. The important factor is self-denial, by which the unity we have in the Holy Spirit becomes visible among us. Our allegiance to all those others who stand united in the Father and the Son by the power of the same Spirit then takes shape and finds its expression.

When Christians relate to each other in love and peace, and stand united in His name, power will emanate from them. A few years ago we had a team who lived in harmony and love, despite various shortcomings. They had contact with a certain couple, and the husband visited the team several times. One evening he told his wife, 'It works, it really works. I saw it with my own eyes. I used to listen when they read to me from the Bible, but I did not believe it, it seemed so unreal. Now I have seen it with my own eyes. Come at once, you must see and feel it yourself!' The man and his entire household were converted and many more of his family followed. He was right: it works!

There are several ways to form a team or group. A team of full-time missionaries or evangelists can work together with the intention of planting a church. Alternatively, people in secular employment can join together to plant a church in their spare time. In either case, the underlying principles remain the same. Attention must be paid to the life of the group itself. As brothers and sisters we need to pray and read the Bible and let ourselves be moulded together by God's love, before we go out into the world. We need to be, in Paul's phraseology, 'a letter from Christ . . . known and read by everybody' (2 Cor 3:3,2).

The power of such a team will make itself felt when we enter into contact with the local population and invite people for a chat. We should live not so much in a glass house as in an open house. An invitation for a cup of coffee can work wonders. We could also set up musical evenings, and there are many other possibilities for meeting people. In the previous chapter I mentioned how our team members became members of social and cultural clubs. They made new contacts and were able to invite their friends to join them for an evening. This led to a whole series of questions being fired at us then, or later, and we were happy to answer them. As Peter has admonished us, 'Always be prepared to give an answer to everyone who asks you to give the reason for the hope that you have' (1 Pet 3:15). Is there a better starting-point than this?

A team serves as a model for the church that is going to be planted. A good team, where love and unity are being developed, will produce a strong church where believers are united in Christ and God's grace reigns supreme. A quarrelling, rebellious team produces a group of people who are also fractious. In the context of BEM activities, we have examples of both.

The home Bible study

A few years ago we had an attractive invitation card printed which read, 'Can we still accept the Twelve Articles of the Christian faith?' It was an invitation to a home Bible study about the gospel. This form of evangelism is particularly effective at the moment:

> A small group of eight to twelve people meeting together informally in homes is the most effective structure for the communication of the gospel in modern seculurban society. Such groups are better suited to the mission of the church in today's urban world than are traditional church services, institutional church programs or the mass communication media.[2]

Another way to get started is to put an advertisement in the local paper. This needs to be done in a way that appeals to people. Some enterprising friends first organised an entertainment evening, during which they suggested a home Bible study. We can also select certain people and invite them by phone. Why should encyclopaedia salesmen be the only ones to do this? We can send invitations by mail or deliver them from door to door, but the most effective way is to invite our friends and acquaintances in person. Clearly, where there is a will, there is a way and we should not give up, even if we are unsuccessful at first. Did you know that Walt Disney failed three times and even went bankrupt before he gave us Mickey Mouse?

The personal approach carries weight. Gert Doornenbal has argued that 'People are helped the most when they are approached individually. Therefore, we should work in small groups. A married couple, for example, can have a home Bible study with another couple.'[3] Some people shy away from the word 'study'. So we may have to find a more suitable name for it. Others, however, may be attracted to the idea of a 'study'.

It is vitally important that home Bible studies should be conducted in the right way. The leader of the group needs to know how to go about it. If he feels uncertain at first, he could invite someone else to lead the first few evenings and observe how things are run. There are a few steps to remember:

1 What is passed on needs to be communicated with enthusiasm. Several times people have said to me, 'You seem to be convinced, don't you?' This has taught me that we do not just pass on a message, we *are* the message. What sort of effect has our message had on our own lives?

2 Everyone needs to be involved in the conversation. The gathering is not a church service with a sermon. People need to react, ask questions and voice their opinions.

3 We need to be aware of the profound effect this method may have. If people are thrilled and convinced at the end of every evening, they will bring along friends and acquaintances the next time. This is how things grow. This is how a church is planted, without the people around us noticing. It bears some similarity to Acts 16, where Lydia pays attention to Paul's words and is converted. From that time onwards her house

becomes the cradle for a new church. Quite a large group had already formed by the time Paul and Silas are imprisoned for throwing out demons, the only thing they did in public in Philippi. When they are miraculously freed from prison, and the jailer and his family have been converted, it is said that 'They went to Lydia's house, where they met with the brothers' (Acts 16:40). We need to keep this in mind when we start out small. God is always willing to surprise us and He makes use of small things in order to achieve great ones.

4   We need to make clear in the Bible study that God has not given His word so that we can turn it into a subject for a debating society. The Bible is never non-committal. Throughout the Book God makes wonderful promises, but He always makes them conditional: 'This is what I shall do, if. . . .' There is a striking example in Jeremiah 11:2,4: 'Listen to the terms of this covenant . . . . Obey me and do everything I command you, and you will be my people, and I will be your God.' At the outset of the Bible study it is important to establish the authority of God's word as our foundation.

5   Normally, our aim is to see a church planted. The steps listed in Chapter 2 apply here as well. However, a home Bible study could exist without there being any intention of planting a church; we then need to watch the size of the group. With a group of twelve or more, it would be appropriate to split up and start a second group. Once these Bible study groups start to multiply, incredible things may happen. John Wesley had all believers meet in small groups. He covered England with them. God has not changed: He is able to do the same again and even more magnificently than before.

Mother and daughter churches

Planting churches in a big city is, perhaps, best be done from within existing churches. We need to accept that the bigger the church the less is achieved by each individual member. A single church cannot reach an entire city; a number of churches, however, scattered over many districts, will bring that goal much closer. There is room for large churches as long as such churches keep in mind that in practice there is a maximum number beyond which it would not be wise to grow. When this number has been reached, we had better plant another church, a daughter church. If we wish to build a 'superchurch', and are reluctant to multiply by division, we are in danger of creating a kingdom of our own. God wishes us to bear fruit as a church as well as individually. That does not mean only increased membership and spiritual growth, but also that new churches will grow from existing churches. The rules that apply here most likely will resemble those of team evangelism.[4]

A new core group needs to be established that will separate from the existing church and start a new one. If an outsider is made responsible for planting a daughter church, he will benefit from spending the first year or so in the mother church. When he knows people well, he is in a position to put forward names of a few people he would like to have in his team. These leaders need to search God's will. The choice needs to be from God, and prayer and fasting will help, as in Acts 13.

The target area where the new church is to be planted is determined in the same way. Only when all the leaders have experienced God's direction in putting together the team can they ask the people chosen to join it. We would do well to ensure that the team members are spiritually mature. The team should consist of three or four married couples and two or three single people from both sexes and from varying age groups. We do not choose people to be members of a church planting team simply because they happen to live in the right area. It might be necessary for some people to consider moving into the target area.

Before someone is asked to join the team, he should show spiritual maturity and suitable spiritual gifts. When we approach these people, it is important to speak frankly about the commitment required. They need to pray first and only then accept this task as the will of God, and be willing to make sacrifices. To sum up, we need divine wisdom and, consequently, prayer and fasting are essential.

Once the team has been formed, we need a plan of action that anticipates developments as clearly as possible. Time is needed for team members in secular employment to get to know each other and prepare themselves for their task. They must free themselves of their commitment to activities in the mother church and get together with the planter of the daughter church once or twice a week for training and prayer. Meanwhile, they are welcome to attend Sunday services at the mother church. Their financial contribution is best given to the newly planted church to prepare materially as well as spiritually. That is why the whole church needs to be informed about this plan and be involved in it. A time will come when an official valedictory service will be needed. The team will then move on and be commended to God for their particular mission. From that moment onwards they begin to function on their own in their new location.

From the beginning it is vital to establish who is to be finally answerable for the new start. If it is the elders of the mother church, they will need an ongoing responsibility enabling them to be in charge. Questions that need answering are: For how long are they answerable? When can the daughter church stand on its own feet?

A few sensitive issues also need to be considered. What guidelines should be made for people who want to leave their home church and join the new church for reasons of their own? Often these people are not an asset to the new church and only want to change churches because of the problems they have created. In turn, they will bring their problems into the new group.

The strain on relations with brothers and sisters who no longer attend the mother church can lead to more serious problems. But is that not what happens in daily living as well?

We have children, raise them and then they leave home. They start a family of their own, and the cycle repeats itself. Solid relationships are of paramount importance and a sign of maturity, but we need to acknowledge that we cannot go through life without growing pains, and that goes for the church of Christ as well. Surely it is a cause for great joy that in planting a new church in this way there is separation without division. In a most positive way, a part is severed from the whole in order to produce new life.

When it is possible to start several churches in one city, we are able to exercise a much greater influence collectively as Christians. Take Brussels, for example. It is divided into nineteen boroughs. We should pray to God and trust that in all these boroughs at least one church will be planted to witness to the fact that Jesus rose from the dead and is alive, though there is enough room, and a need, for more than nineteen new churches. In every district, in every densely populated part of the city, there could and should be such a witness.

This holds true for other cities as well. In this era of urbanisation we need to direct our efforts towards highly populated areas. We need to be where the people are. Existing churches would benefit from adopting this strategy. When it is suggested that the mother church will be weaker if we let people join a new church, I reply, 'Do you realise how empty chairs can boost the morale of those left behind? A mother church can be compared with a young mother who has just had a baby and has to recover her strength—she will eventually.' Judging from the examples I have seen in different situations, churches generally do recover after being drained that way.

Evangelistic visits

When we find other Christians with a desire to plant a church, one sure way to get started is to pay evangelistic visits. Often we have reversed the command of Jesus Christ, 'Go into all the world and preach the good news to all creation' (Mk 16:15), by turning this 'go' evangelism into 'come' evangelism. We invite people to attend a Sunday service, to come and hear the preacher, to come and join this or that, but Jesus said, 'Go.' We need to visit people and build up relationships and introduce them to Jesus Christ.

At our disposal is a full range of methods to help us to come into contact with people. When new people move into your neighbourhood, for example, pay them a welcome visit and see if you can help out in any way, with practical help or advice about shops, schools, etc. You will be surprised to see how much this is appreciated. New residential areas are being developed. This offers the opportunity to visit at an early stage. In *I Believe in Church Growth* Eddie Gibbs gives a wonderful testimony from the Revd Jess Yates of Bamford Chapel, Rochdale:

> Just over a year ago a visitation was carried out on the newest estate in the community. Before the visitation not one family came to our church from the estate. One good contact was made and followed up. Now twelve couples and their seventeen children are integrated into our fellowship.[5]

Another type of person we could visit are those who are in distress. They would welcome a gesture of love and compassion. A family might have experienced trouble or conflict; when we hear about it, we could pay a visit and show we care. We could also seek out friends or acquaintances and show our concern for them.

A leader in one of our churches told me, 'The best way to make contacts is to have a baby and to work on my allotment.' His wife made contact with other women by showing off their new baby, and he shared his 'weed philosophy' with the other men: 'What happens when you do not tend your garden for a whole year? . . . What do you think is the reason? Why does the world not improve by itself?' In this way he steered the conversation to the truth that all things this side of eternity are subject to death and decay. Nothing improves all by itself. On the contrary, things naturally get worse and worse. He made for himself an opportunity to speak about sin, its origins and its consequences.

A hospital visit is another great opportunity. When people come face to face with the frailty and transience of life, many start thinking about their own lives.

There are many other ways to call on people. You might want to visit the parents of children who have been to the children's club, or people whom you have met at a wedding or funeral, or at an entertainment evening or cultural event. It would be a good idea to start a personal card catalogue of all the people we have visited and might want to visit again. This is how Evangelism Explosion works. The idea is to develop 'warmer' contacts in the first place, and 'colder' ones later, with the intention of interesting them in the gospel. When we put together a visiting schedule with several others jointly, 'Combined preparation and follow-up activities is indispensable. The study of the Scriptures and prayer will be an important part of this.'[6] The way we go about these visits is very important.

At this point I would like to list a few suggestions that could be helpful:

1 Pay several calls on the same person.

2 Be sure to keep the call short for the first time—fifteen minutes will do.

3 Try not to betray people's trust and avoid passing on confidential information.

4 Take a copy of the Bible, but not too conspicuously.

5 Avoid pious talk and listen carefully.

6 Be prepared to go overtime, but do not impose on people while talking about Christ's love for them.

7 Do not be shy about the actual reason for your visit—to tell people about the love of Christ.

8 Prepare for your visit by reading your 'contact cards' and

bringing these people and their concerns before God.

9 Dress well.

10 Concentrate on asking questions, not on presenting doctrine.

11 Do not be tempted to get into arguments.

12 Try to pass on God's message in the appropriate way.

13 Keep in mind you might want to visit again!

14 Give an invitation to a special event at your church.

15 Leave some literature.

We need to plan our visiting schedules carefully. When you want to speak to a couple, try to see them together. We need to ask God for entire families, since these are the building blocks for a church.

In whatever way we are involved in church planting evangelism, we have to see the task through to the end. There is no quick and easy way to spiritual success. It is a struggle that needs to be conducted in the spirit of love, wearing the armour of faith. We need to share our lives and everything that God has given us. That takes time, but ultimately it will have value for eternity.

Notes

[1] C. Peter Wagner, *Your Church Can Grow: Seven Vital Signs of a Healthy Church* (Regal Books: Ventura, California, 1984), p 163.

[2] Howard A. Snyder, *The Problem of Wineskins: Church Structure in a Technological Age* (Inter-Varsity Press: Downers Grove, Illinois, 1976), p 139.

[3] Quoted in Leen La Riviere, 'Succesvol evangeliseren', in *Evangelisatie*, ed Leen La Riviere (J. H. Kok: Kampen, 1980), p 70.

[4] This is the subject of Ben Sawatski's 'Church Planting with Mother Churches: A Step-by-Step Guide for Starting a Church', Special Lecture Belgian Evangelical Mission, Brussels, 15–17 March 1982. In this series of papers Sawatski deals with such related subjects as 'The Role of the Mother Church in Church

Planting', 'Launching a New Church', 'Infant Church Planting Situations', etc.

[5] Eddie Gibbs, *I Believe in Church Growth* (Hodder & Stoughton: London, 1985), p 148.

[6] La Riviere, *op cit,* p 45.

7

Church Planting: Love as a Method

Some friends once took me to a prayer meeting in England. It was very lively, to the point of being noisy. People seemed to think that God was deaf! By God's grace I have learned to love all kinds of Christians, but that evening I could feel myself becoming antagonistic. I decided to ask some pertinent questions when the prayer meeting was over. We had coffee and something to eat, and then I launched my offensive. I asked one person present if he was involved in evangelism. He was very modest but replied that every Friday night, after prayers, they went to the redlight district to talk to the prostitutes and their clients, and try to preach the gospel. 'Last week,' the man said, 'I met a Polish man there. We could not understand one another, but I got him a cup of coffee and sat with him for an hour.' 'Why did you do that?' I asked, dumbfounded. 'Well, just to love sinners as Jesus did, remember?'

That night I lay on my bed, thinking over his words, 'to love sinners as Jesus did, remember?' Of course I remembered what Jesus did, but was I practising it? This question kept running through my mind. The next evening I had to travel from Bristol to London by train. As I was getting on to the platform, my attention was drawn by a scruffily dressed man. He appeared to be drunk and was desperately trying to make contact with the other travellers. Nobody wanted to have anything to do with him. Finally, he came up to me and offered me a cigarette. 'No, thanks, I don't smoke,' I answered, but I

113

added instantly, 'It's very kind of you all the same.' That was the signal. 'Then I'll get you a cup of coffee on the train,' he replied. When the train pulled in, he insisted on finding two seats near the dining-car.

When he arrived with the coffee, there was more of it in the saucer than in the cup. That is to be expected when a drunk carries a cup of coffee in a moving train! Most drunks talk loudly, but he was exceptionally loud. I asked his name and he asked mine, but since Johan was too difficult to pronounce, he announced to all who wanted to hear that he had renamed me 'Johnny boy'. Gradually I tried to direct the conversation towards the meaning of life and of what Christ did for us. That was when the noise really started. Swinging his arms violently and roaring like a wounded lion, he made it clear to me that he would have none of such nonsense.

The ticket collector was also dragged into the conversation when he came along: 'Are you a religious man, too? You can't be!' I did not seem to be making much progress and the journey was to last about two hours. Everyone in our compartment was observing us. Suddenly, I remembered the words I had heard the evening before: 'Just to love sinners as Jesus did, remember?'

It was then that I understood what God had been trying to teach me, and I started to pray silently for that man. Meanwhile, he told me he sometimes saw prostitutes. When I asked what he did for a living, he replied, 'I steal for a living, but I only steal from those who won't miss it when it's gone.' All of this in his bellowing voice. I just prayed and God began to give me love. I lost my sense of embarrassment and adjusted to his company, even though I could not tell him about Jesus Christ. When we arrived in London, he said, 'Shall I carry your suitcase for you?' I replied, 'Sure, as long as you don't steal it!' He staggered out of the train with it, bumping into people as he went, and swore heavily. Finally, he put it down and said, 'Sorry, Johnny boy, I shouldn't have sworn, I probably hurt your feelings and I didn't mean to.'

He ran off into the crowd and left me standing utterly amazed. Had God's Spirit done such a work in his heart as to make him sensitive? To love sinners as Jesus did, remember?

Loving instead of preaching

It is much easier to preach to sinners than to love them. I know that from experience. It could be one of the main reasons for stagnation in many churches and individual Christians. Donald McGavran, the father of church growth studies, has observed that:

> Some congregations and denominations get 'stuck' because they are such 'good' Christians that they isolate themselves from outsiders. . . . Rather, the Christian must multiply contact with the world while remaining separate and holy. Christians must not be so separated and so holy that they flinch every time they see a sinner. They must establish cordial, friendly and genuine relationships. This is where new converts shine. . . . New converts have many contacts in 'the world.' These contacts comprise a great reservoir of non-Christians to whom the new converts can witness.[1]

We need to learn what it means to be in the world but not of the world. Paul was 'a shepherd of souls, sent into the world, not to lecture sinners, but to love them. . . . Love made Paul warm-hearted and affectionate in his evangelism.'[2] Today we tend to emphasise plans and programmes, but they will not produce fruit if they are not done in the spirit of love. Our motives outweigh our actions. What is it that moves us to evangelise, and in which spirit do we go about it? Again, according to Packer:

> Such was evangelism according to Paul: going out in love, as Christ's agent in the world, to teach sinners the truth of the gospel with a view to converting and saving them. If, therefore, we are engaging in this activity, and with this aim, we are evangelizing,

irrespective of the particular means by which we are doing it.[3]

We need to learn afresh that the essence of the good news is love. God gave us His Son out of love—His *only* Son: 'And for the Son, in incarnating that love, it meant renouncing His own right of living and giving His life for the world. Only in this light—when the Son is put in place of the world—can one even begin to understand the cross.'[4] Jesus Christ, whom we have chosen to follow, has shown in His life and death the full breadth and depth of love. The disciples had a close-up view:

> They saw how their Master denied Himself many of the comforts and pleasures of the world and became a servant among them. They saw how the things which they cherished—physical satisfaction, popular acclaim, prestige—He refused; while the things which they sought to escape—poverty, humiliation, sorrow, and even death—He accepted willingly for their sake.[5]

We should begin to think about saving the lost in this same spirit. An example from history is that of the Moravian Brethren who in humility gave up everything they had and spread out all over the world. Their motivation was the love of God through Jesus Christ and love for their fellow men. They considered that their lives were not their own, made sacrifices gladly and conquered large areas of the world for Jesus Christ. Here, in the cold, intellectual West, we believe we can solve everything by discussion and debate. But, as Derek Copley points out, 'I know that if I lose an argument then I've lost it. But I can win an argument and still be the loser.'[6] Love finds its way to the heart when the mind cannot do so. Apparently, Napoleon once said, 'There's only one way not to be defeated by love and that is to run from it.'[7] Love takes away tension, it is disarming. It melts away antagonism, just like sunshine melting the snow. 1 Corinthians 13, the song in praise of love, tells us, 'it is not self-seeking' (v 5).

Love, moreover, is resourceful! As David Prior observes,

'love will, of course, find many creative and imaginative ways to come alongside those who are strangers to God. The love of Christ controlling a local church will drive its members out all the time in sustained evangelism.'[8] We need to turn to God in humility and ask His forgiveness for our callous hearts, for our self-centred lives, for our cold hands that do not bear the marks of the labour of love. Then we need to offer up our lives and say, 'Lord God, please fill me with your love. Let your Spirit fill and flow through my heart.' If we do that in faith, we shall be amazed to see how God is able to use our words and deeds.

The down-to-earth church

Love has infinitely more to do with our will than with our feelings. The will to love comes first, feelings come after. This means that in a very concrete way, and led by God's Spirit, we have more contact with the world. Terry Virgo talks about a church leader who hired a local wine bar and invited his contacts to a meal: 'Most of those invited had first been befriended at the local golf club which he and his church members have infiltrated with considerable gospel impact.'[9] We can freely function as Christians in a whole range of clubs, sports clubs and community centres. In this way we are able to contribute to the community. Through our lifestyle and friendship we can begin passing on the good news of the greatest and deepest love of all times.

Getting to know someone who is ready to receive the gospel often opens doors to a whole group of people. The society we live in is formed in the shape of a web:

People movements take a number of forms. In the first place, there is the 'follow-my-leader' model. . . . We also read of *crowd conversions*. . . . There are a number of instances of *household conversion* [and] . . . community decisions. . . . The fifth pattern is that of a web movement.'[10]

Just as the threads of a web are interconnected, so people are linked to each other by many kinds of relationships. They form groups—within the family, in cultural and community centres with other colleagues at work, in sports clubs etc. By mutual links of this kind, it is possible not only to reach an individual person, but also an entire group.

Sociologists maintain that the average individual has about fifty people in his circle of friends and acquaintances. So one personal contact may lead to a contact with an entire circle. We saw this when the conversion of a few train drivers resulted in several other drivers finding Christ. Many times this has happened in families: 'More people are brought to Christ by the life and witness of another Christian than by the ministry of crusades, missions, campaigns and the like.'[11]

Church growth specialists have observed 'the homogeneous unit principle' as one of the chief reasons for the success of fast-growing churches. By this they mean that 'people want to be Christians without, however, crossing the boundaries of race, language or social class.'[12] They conclude, therefore, that we need to address a particular class of the population, so, for instance, a professional or businessman's church might come into being. I must admit that I have difficulty with this principle. I can see it might be psychologically and sociologically advisable in the sense that less resistance needs to be overcome in order to bring people together in a church where they meet others like themselves. But we need to be wary of basing our strategy on human wisdom. The task we have been given is to reach all people. Numerical success is not the standard by which we measure our ministry. The Bible says that we are 'all sons of God through faith in Christ Jesus. . . . There is neither Jew nor Greek, slave nor free, male nor female, for you are all one in Christ Jesus' (Gal 3:26,28). I would rather believe in God on account of a church that represents all of the population. Such a church is a foretaste of the future, a manifestation of the fellowship that only God can bring about.

Far or Near?

In God's strength we are free to love sinners; this, however, means that we need to get to know them. We must learn to see people as God sees them. Ralph Norton, founder of the Belgian Evangelical Mission, chose as his motto, 'See it from God's point of view.' The word 'sinner' does not refer only to drunks and adulterers. There are 'clean' sinners as well, and they need to be saved just as much. A sinner is anyone who has not arrived at a simple faith in Jesus Christ and a total devotion to Him (Jn 16:8–9). The gospel shows how some religious leaders were more hardened as sinners than tax collectors. We should not be fooled by appearances. High standards of morality do not make someone a Christian; that person may still be living a rebellious life. In the spirit of love we must try to win sinners for Christ for the sake of their eternal salvation.

We need to understand where people are in relation to Christ. Some have no awareness of Christianity. They have a completely atheistic background and their thinking is far removed from the good news. Others have been raised in a Christian family, or have heard somehow about the Christian faith, but have not yet understood the personal implications. As Voltaire once put it, with reference to his relationship with Christ, 'We say hello, but we don't talk.'[13] Yet others have heard all they need and just have to be encouraged to make a decision. We can present these different positions in a scale that indicates where people are. This scale was developed by James Engel of the Wheaton Graduate School.[14]

WHERE IS THIS PEOPLE IN
THEIR MOVEMENT TOWARDS CHRIST?
The Engel Scale

No Awareness of Christianity −7

Awareness of the Existence of Chrisianity −6

Some Knowledge of the Gospel −5

Understanding of the Fundamentals of the Gospel −4

Grasp of the Personal Implications −3

Recognition of Personal Need −2

Challenge and Decision to Receive Christ −1

—Conversion—

Evaluation of the Decision +1

Incorporation into a Fellowship of Christians +2

Active Propagators of the Gospel +3

The purpose of this scale is to assist us in our efforts to bring people to faith in Christ. We first need to learn where they are. Clearly, not everyone will be approached in the same manner. As a young Christian I learned my lesson. In my fervour and love for the Lord I witnessed to everyone I met. Once I spent twenty minutes explaining the gospel to a certain man, after which he said, 'Not bad at all, brother.' He was obviously a Christian! I should have asked some questions and listened to him to find out where he stood in relation to Christ.

About the scale Edward R. Dayton observes:

The important thing in all of this is not the scale itself but the understanding that people do have movement towards Christ, and we need to have some way of knowing where they are on the journey so that we can speak to them at their point of need.[15]

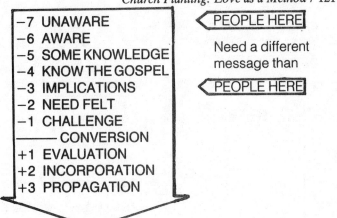

The idea behind the scale helped, but there were a few elements missing all the same, so a few changes and improvements were made. In *What's Gone Wrong with the Harvest?* the scheme is further developed:

> It appears, then, that the Great Commission contains three related but distinctly different communication mandates: (1) *to proclaim* the message; (2) *to persuade* the unbeliever; and (3) *to cultivate* the believer. . . . The figure on the next page is of critical significance, because it represents an attempt to place these communication ministries in the perspective of the spiritual decision process that is followed as one becomes a believer in Jesus Christ and grows in the faith.[16]

A lot of love and patience is needed to reach people for God's kingdom. However, when we receive a clear picture of the point at which they have arrived in their relationship to Christ, this will help us to witness effectively—that is, in a manner adapted to them.

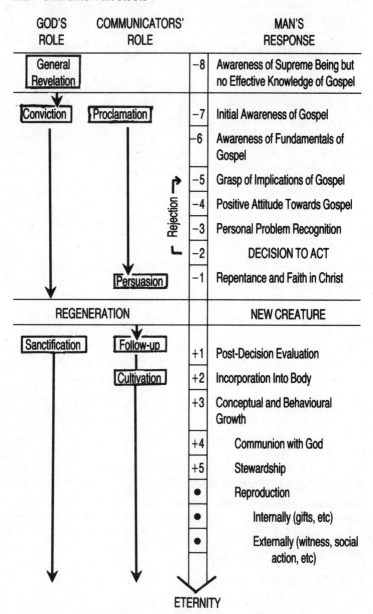

The Spiritual Decision Process

Degrees of resistance

Another factor is of some importance. Not everyone is eager to receive the gospel. Some people have been hardened against the good news by past experiences or prejudice. You touch a sore spot when you mention God's name. Love, however, is able to reach them, and even if it is discouraged at first, it will live up to its reputation that 'it is not easily angered, it keeps no record of wrongs' (1 Cor 13:5). This problem has been studied and a scale of degrees of resistance and receptivity has been made.

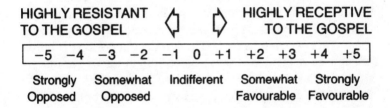

RESISTANCE/RECEPTIVITY SCALE

HIGHLY RESISTANT TO THE GOSPEL							HIGHLY RECEPTIVE TO THE GOSPEL

−5	−4	−3	−2	−1	0	+1	+2	+3	+4	+5

Strongly Opposed	Somewhat Opposed	Indifferent	Somewhat Favourable	Strongly Favourable

Some people know about the gospel, yet they rebel against it. They may have an inaccurate understanding of it, carrying around with them a distorted image from their education, or perhaps from contact with sects, or they may have heard anything but the truth in church! To them the gospel is bad news. When we track down the causes and listen patiently to their story—when people have an opportunity to unburden their hearts—this in itself could be an opportunity to tell the good news.

Everyone needs an approach adapted to his own personality. Love has to lead us and show the way. In other words, we are not to talk like a jammed record player and give the same line to everyone we meet. The gospel is God's answer to human need. In the final account, all our problems can be traced back to our broken relationship with our Creator. Recovery in Christ remains the basic answer for all situations. We can classify human needs into several categories. There seems to be a relationship between the concerns and problems people wrestle with and their social position. Maslow has illustrated these needs in a pyramid, showing how people relate to needs (see chart opposite). Joseph Aldrich has helped us by turning Maslow's 'Hierarchy of Needs' into an instrument we can use to see how to acquaint people with the gospel. The idea is then to provide an answer to the particular felt need from our experience of a living relationship with Christ. This is the way of love, and therefore very effective and patently Christian.[18]

According to Aldrich, it is Maslow's belief that 'although all of these needs are intrinsic to the human family, not all of them are on center stage at the same time.'[19] In introducing the second pyramid he says, 'The serving dimension of church life can be expanded if these basic human needs are understood and met. Notice how man's needs are opportunities for us to share God's solution as you study the chart on p.126.'[20]

It is easier to meet the needs of people at the bottom of the pyramid than to meet those of people at the top. Therefore, the next chart (p.127) may help us to see how. 'To evangelize the weak, the Christian comes to find and meet a need. To reach the strong, self-assured person, progress comes by involving him in meeting *someone else's need*.'[21] When we set about winning people for Christ, it is essential that we carefully consider these realities, and in so doing make the best of the chances we have. We need to fight the battle strategically.

These schemes might seem complicated, but the basic principle is love. It is rather like a very young mother with a baby. We may think she will not be able to look after the baby, but in actual fact 'mother love' finds a way, and we are amazed to see how good she is at it. When the love of Christ fills our lives, that love will find its way to the hearts of others. That

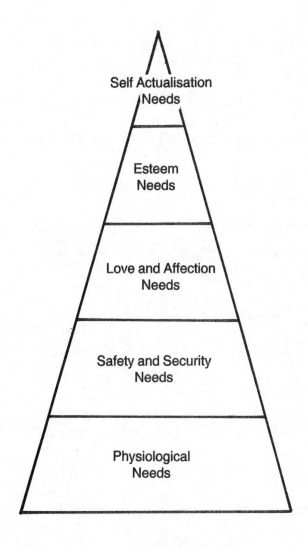

First Scheme

Man's Need

God's Solution

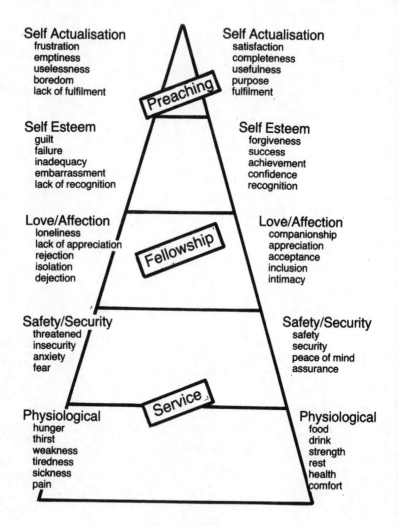

Self Actualisation
frustration
emptiness
uselessness
boredom
lack of fulfilment

Self Actualisation
satisfaction
completeness
usefulness
purpose
fulfilment

Preaching

Self Esteem
guilt
failure
inadequacy
embarrassment
lack of recognition

Self Esteem
forgiveness
success
achievement
confidence
recognition

Love/Affection
loneliness
lack of appreciation
rejection
isolation
dejection

Love/Affection
companionship
appreciation
acceptance
inclusion
intimacy

Fellowship

Safety/Security
threatened
insecurity
anxiety
fear

Safety/Security
safety
security
peace of mind
assurance

Service

Physiological
hunger
thirst
weakness
tiredness
sickness
pain

Physiological
food
drink
strength
rest
health
comfort

Second Scheme

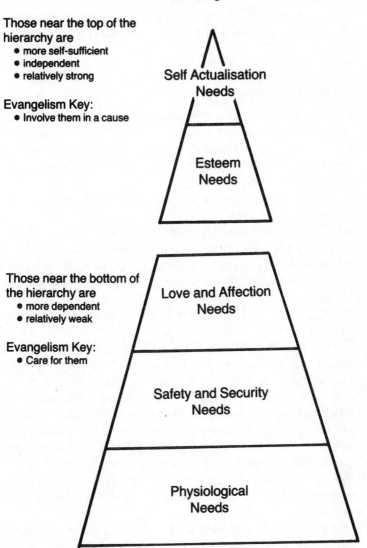

Those near the top of the hierarchy are
- more self-sufficient
- independent
- relatively strong

Evangelism Key:
- Involve them in a cause

Self Actualisation Needs

Esteem Needs

Those near the bottom of the hierarchy are
- more dependent
- relatively weak

Evangelism Key:
- Care for them

Love and Affection Needs

Safety and Security Needs

Physiological Needs

Third Scheme

love, however, also leads us to take the trouble to understand the other person, and be of service as effectively as possible in Christ's name.

Circumstances considered

Human life does not always run smoothly. We go up to the mountain tops and then down into the valleys. Sometimes we are more open to changes than at other times. We should not overlook these circumstances as we try to help people on the basis of the gospel.

There is an increased openness when people move house, change jobs, experience divorce, bereavement, serious accident, disease or unemployment. When people marry or have a baby they are also more open to change. In other words, in sad as well as in happy circumstances, there is an increasing receptivity. These are times when entirely new things happen which are emotionally uprooting. Things certain and familiar disappear. New problems need to be solved and new decisions need to be taken.

Young adults are more likely to be receptive than people in middle age, who are more settled in their ways. When people get married and have a baby, serious questions are raised. Life takes them by surprise and forces them to be responsible. Young adulthood is the time when most of us are open to serious thought as to how we can make the most of this life. From the point of view of church planting evangelism, this group is particularly interesting, for it provides magnificent building blocks for the church. Young families possess a special power of attraction for others, and provide us with a start for child and teenage evangelism.

All kinds of influences make people receptive to new ideas. We should aim to reach people who influence others, people who are naturally more inclined towards new things and know how to pass them on to others around them. 'Opinion makers' we could call them. In order to make a start, it is vital to discover these people first and begin with them. Then, humanly speaking, we have a better chance to succeed. Especially in villages or smaller communities this seems to be an element of great importance.

I know of a village where there was a born leader. When he put his mind to playing soccer, he would have the majority of the neighbourhood playing soccer within six months. A Bible study was started in his home. When he asked a question one evening and was invited to formulate a reply all by himself, he not only came up with the right answer, but also added, 'You see, in a little while I'll be able to tell them myself.' Although this was said jokingly, that was exactly what happened later.

Sociologists have taught us that society can be divided into five different categories with regard to our reactions to new habits or ideas. The first are the *innovators*. Of themselves they will produce new ideas and are very open to suggestions from others. The second are the *early adaptors*. They are quick to adopt anything new, without wanting to be the first. They do not take the initiative but become advocates of new ideas relatively early and adapt quite easily and quickly. The third group consists of the *early majority*. They are somewhat slower in following new habits or ideas, but are not too difficult to convince. They will only come round when they see that many others have taken to a new idea or habit. The fourth group consists of the *late majority*. It takes a long time for them to adopt new ideas. In fact, they would rather not. They are reluctant at first, but will follow suit when they see that the great majority has adopted them. The last group consists of the *procrastinators*. They are at the opposite end to the innovators. They resist any kind of change and are more problem-oriented than possibility-oriented. They are, in fact, the pessimists.

The proportions in this diagram are important. Innovators and procrastinators are rare breeds. Most of us are somewhere in the middle. Of course, it is good policy to start with the innovators when we get the chance. In their turn, they will set others alight and the word of God will spread quickly.

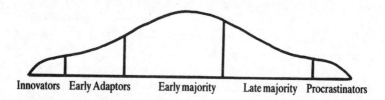

Innovators | Early Adaptors | Early majority | Late majority | Procrastinators

Closing comments

I have intentionally gathered together these schemes, techniques and methods in the chapter that deals with the motive of love. Cold calculations will not be of any use if we are not motivated by the love of God. We should not just look around us and inquire: 'Where are our people? How do sociologists or psychologists classify them so that we know how to reach them?' We also need to look inside ourselves and let the light of God's love shine in our hearts, so that we warm to others and are able to call Christ's compassion our own.

Scripture says that 'When he saw the crowds, he had compassion on them, because they were harassed and helpless, like sheep without a shepherd' (Mt 9:36). We should examine our hearts. Are we a faithful picture of what Christ had in mind when He spoke of people belonging to Him? Is my life, is our life in fellowship a stumbling-block for the gospel? We should not only look around and inside us, but also to God who desires to bless and save people. He loves them more than any other creature in His entire universe. Moreover, He is able to work powerfully by His Spirit and break hard hearts and melt down resistance. He is able and willing to make Himself known, when we go forward into the spiritual battle by faith, trusting Him. What do we expect of Him? If the principle of 'may it be according to your faith' were applied to you, what would happen? Faith is necessary to please God. This is what He blesses richly—'faith expressing itself through love' (Gal 5:6).

Notes

1. Donald A. McGavran and Winfield C. Arn, *Ten Steps for Church Growth* (Harper & Row: San Francisco, 1977), pp 83–84.
2. J. I. Packer, *Evangelism and the Sovereignty of God* (Inter-Varsity Press: Downers Grove, Illinois, 1961), pp 51–52.
3. *ibid*, p 53.
4. Robert E. Coleman, *The Master Plan of Evangelism* (Fleming H. Revell: Old Tappan, New Jersey, 1982), p 62.
5. *ibid*, pp 62–63.
6. Derek and Nancy Copley, *Building with Bananas: People Problems in the Church* (Paternoster Press: Exeter, 1984), p 78.
7. Quoted in Arthur McPhee, *Vriendschapevangelisatie*, trans R. Van Essen (Gideon: Hoornaar, nd), p 55. My own translation; the original in English, *Friendship Evangelism* (Zondervan: Grand Rapids, Michigan, 1978) is out of print and cannot be traced.
8. David Prior, *Bedrock: A Vision for the Local Church* (Hodder & Stoughton: London, 1985), p 80.
9. Terry Virgo, *Restoration in the Church* (Kingsway Publications: Eastbourne, 1985), p 103.
10. Eddie Gibbs, *I Believe in Church Growth* (Hodder & Stoughton: London, 1985), p 96.
11. Gordon Jones, *The Church Without Walls: A Workbook for the Local Church* (Marshalls: Basingstoke, 1985), p 74.
12. Bram Krol, *Gemeentegroei* (Buiten, Schipperheyn: Amsterdam, 1982), p 47.
13. Quoted in McPhee, *op cit*, p 81.
14. Edward Dayton, *That Everyone May Hear: Reaching the Unreached* (MARC: Monrovia, California, 1980), p 43.
15. *ibid*, p 46.
16. James F. Engel and Wilbert Norton, *What's Gone Wrong with the Harvest?* (Zondervan: Grand Rapids, Michigan, 1982), pp 44–45. This model, as presented here, has undergone an interesting history. In rudimentary forms, it was first suggested by Viggo Sogaard while he was a student in the Wheaton Graduate School. Later it was revised by James F. Engel and published in such sources as *Church Growth Bulletin* and elsewhere during 1973.

Since that time, modifications have been introduced as others have made suggestions. Particularly helpful comments have been advanced by Richard Senzig of the communications faculty at the Wheaton Graduate School and Professors C. Peter Wagner and Charles Kraft of the Fuller School of World Mission. (Engel and Norton's n 3, pp 44–45.)

[17] Dayton, *op cit,* p 47.

[18] The three schemes that follow have been taken, with permission, from Joseph C. Aldrich, *Life-Style Evangelism* (Multnomah Press: Portland, Oregon, 1981).

[19] *ibid,* p 91.

[20] *ibid,* p 94.

[21] *ibid,* p 96.

8

Church Planting: Avoiding Mistakes

Speaking from our experience in church planting for the past twenty-five years, we ourselves have made quite a few mistakes and have seen others make futher errors. When learning to skate you are bound to fall and see others falling. The difference, of course, is that mistakes made on the evangelistic skating rink have far-reaching consequences. We therefore need to help each other avoid certain things which lead to failure. For a Christian there is only one way to do it right, and a thousand ways to do it wrong! We cannot deal here with all possible mistakes, but a number of common ones can be avoided.

A bad example

When a number of Christians want to start a church, and their private lives are a poor example, the result of their work will reflect this weakness. The same principle is at work in raising children: they will not so much do as we say, but do as we ourselves do. Our example will be followed, not our words. It might seem unnecessary to say this, but experience teaches us differently. This is one of the most common obstacles to the growth of a new church.

In one particular case, the members of a church planting training team were caught up time and again in the same dispute. When they started out on their visits, one of them would say, 'We first need a time of prayer before we go.' Someone else would reply, 'It's too late for that right now.' 'But if we don't pray first, God won't be able to bless us.' 'Pray when you're on your way.' 'It just doesn't work that way: I can't concentrate.' 'Then we'll pray when we're back here.' That, of course, was not right either, because prayer was needed beforehand, and so on. You could not say that there were serious conflicts, just minor differences of opinion. Today I could take you to the small church that they planted. You can guess what you would find there: minor differences of opinion and a pastor trying to reconcile them. We reap what we sow.

Peter Cotterell has said that 'It is commonly recognized that behaviour inappropriate to the claims of Christianity serves to cancel out the proclamation of the message of God when made in propositions.'[1] This inappropriate behaviour could be anything from family arguments or telling lies to unfaithfulness in marriage. It could be related to the purity of our motives, which will be recognised faster than we think. Are we servants, like the One we profess to follow? We should not dodge the test of God's word for our own lives, and we might be in need of advice from an observant friend.

A false start

When a new church is just beginning, there are particular dangers. A bad start often means a bad race. The original cell will determine the end result. We would like to direct your attention to three possible dangers:

First, a predominance of underprivileged people in the initial phase. By this we mean people with problems which they largely create themselves by the way they live. These people are in constant need of our attention. The gospel is a message of love, and we have to accept one another as we are. We are called to serve and help one another. People are drawn to us because we can help them. Often they do not have a clear understanding of the gospel but like to come to church because we take them seriously. Then these people bring their friends. In this way we end up with a group of socially unadapted people. Other people who might like to join will not do so. They are likely to get the idea that the church is only for 'misfits' and not for them. Moreover, they are ill at ease among those less fortunate than themselves and have not yet acquired the God-given grace to mix with them.

This group requires a lot of attention, with the result that the church planter soon spends all his time following them closely and clearing up their problems. If the church wants to defend the weak, it should first become a church. There is a limit to what the cell group can do. It is wise, therefore, to delay inviting this group to join the church and to wait until it has grown to a certain size. However, on a personal level we are free to help some of them. When others join the church, they will learn from this sort of personal ministry and grow to assist in the church's mission to the weaker ones. If we do not act in this way, we will remain a small group of isolated people.

Second, 'religion freaks' form another problem group. A few years ago, when we started a new work in a small city, we found a group of people ready to 'follow the Bible'. After a while things stagnated; there was no growth. We did not understand why at first, until we discovered one of the families had been connected with the Jehovah Witnesses before we arrived, and another was involved first with the Mormons and later with an Eastern sect. A third family had been involved with three different sects before they joined us. Most of this city of 15,000 inhabitants knew perfectly well that these families were always eager to pass on the latest religion they had embraced. That is why we were not getting anywhere.

Since then we ask many more questions when we first approach people and go and visit them in their own home for Bible teaching. We are no longer in such a hurry to tell them, 'Come to our church, come to the service.'

Third, a concentration of young people may also present a

problem. Some people think we should start by reaching teenagers. The cry 'When you have youth, you have the future,' can still be heard loud and clear. Once we found ourselves facing the problem that we had twenty to twenty-five youngsters but no one to direct them. They sincerely wanted to follow Christ but, in addition to the usual problems experienced by adolescents, they were the only Christians in their families.

Some parents were indifferent or unable to help. Some strongly objected to their children becoming Christians. 'We wish you had stayed with your old friends' (regulars at bars or drug users), one son was told. The worst thing was that these young Christians had no family to go to to pour out their hearts, and relax by listening to Christian music. This state of affairs finally took care of itself when some of the youngsters grew up and married.

It was difficult to attract married couples to join this church because they thought it was only for teenagers. From the start it is advisable to concentrate on a particular target group. Gene Getz believes that 'the primary target for evangelism should be adults and consequently whole households.'[2]

One half of a couple

A predicament common in Europe is that one part of a family is won for Christ and the other part lags behind. In some cases the church is nearly exclusively made up of women. Elsewhere, men might predominate. This produces some serious problems for the people involved as well as for the congregation. Robert Scott-Cook has observed that 'As soon as Crispus believed, all his household was reached. This was a key factor in New Testament evangelism.'[3] The Book of Acts abounds with examples of this.

The way in which we try to pass on the gospel could determine whether we reach families, or parts of families. We need to develop an appropriate method that targets entire families. I once met a lady who told me that her husband would almost certainly not be interested in receiving the gospel. She wanted to learn more and invited my wife along at a time when he was not around. I intentionally disregarded this suggestion and came at a time when he was sure to be there. He accepted Jesus before his wife did! In cities, we have adopted the habit of working with questionnaires in order to make new contacts. When the husband or wife alone is interested in hearing the gospel, we ask, 'Could we come again when your husband (or wife) is at home?' The time of day is also important. When we wish to win families for Christ we should visit when most of the family, especially parents, can reasonably be expected to be home. Melvin Hodge holds that 'when a person accepts Christ, all attention of counsellors should go to the effort to bring the whole family to Christ.'[4] In prayer and faith we need to reach towards that goal. Pray for families, not individuals.

Sounding different

Church planting is often carried out by foreign missionaries, coming from another culture and language background. They might speak the same language but come from another region and bring their own accent and habits. There is reason to rejoice and be thankful when foreigners proclaim the truths of the gospel. More often than not they have made sacrifices to come to us. They should realise, however, that the new church should have a local flavour and a regional accent. When we leave our native soil we have to keep this in mind.

In one of our larger cities I was invited to preach in the Sunday morning service. It was led by a local man, but he had been thoroughly trained by an American missionary. His behaviour was not natural, and issued from entirely different customs and a different culture. I had the feeling that I was in a church in America, the only difference being that no English was spoken. This kind of thing could impede growth, as David

Burnett has pointed out:

> It was, however, Melvin Hodge who popularised the use of the
> term 'indigenous' as it applied to church planting. Hodge
> described an indigenous church as one that is 'a native church . . .
> which shares the life of the country in which it is planted, and finds
> within itself the ability to govern itself, support itself, and repro-
> duce itself.'[5]

More recently, other mission specialists have felt this statement to be incomplete and have argued instead that 'all the
three selfs could be in full operation but the church could still
be a foreign institution, considered by the nationals as a weird
and irrelevant curiosity in their society.'[6] If a church is to have
a chance to grow, it needs to be well rooted in the Scriptures,
but also in the immediate environment. Most Sunday services
in Spain start rather late—it is part of their Southern heritage.
In Great Britain 11 am seems to be the sacred starting time
and in some parts of the Netherlands all believers are in their
pews a full ten minutes before the service. We might think
these things are of little importance, but they are expressions
of local character and make local people feel at home.

False emphasis

Another obstacle which might hinder the growth of a church is
that some leaders are too fond of riding their favourite hobby
horse. Their preaching comes around to the same subject
nearly every time. In this way we identify maranatha people,
kingdom people, 'baptism in the Spirit' people, and so on.
Whichever text they choose, they will always come back to
their favourite topic. Usually they feel strongly about their
subject, have studied it thoroughly and are able to answer any
questions about it.

The great need today, however, is to proclaim 'the whole
will of God' (Acts 20:27). We need to acquaint believers as

quickly as possible with the entire Bible and with Christian doctrine. We need to help them feed themselves with the word and build them up into stable, balanced Christians, able to help others.

An evangelist was once put to work as a church planter. After two and a half years, the congregation told him, 'Everything you preach we have already heard three times.' He answered in the right spirit and said, 'You're right. I'm an evangelist, not a teacher. It's time for me to go.' Now the church is growing again under the leadership of capable elders.

Untrained soldiers

If we do not train for battle the people God has given us, we shall leave behind a nursery of spiritual babies instead of adults wearing God's suit of armour. We need to distinguish between teaching and training. Teaching means passing on information to people. It is possible to attend a Bible study for years and still be a spiritual weakling. Training involves practising what you have been taught so that you become useful. Faith is like a muscle, and muscles need exercise. Believers need to be helped to discover their gifts and learn how to use them. From the start, they need to take part in spreading the gospel. They will have to understand that they are saved 'to do good works, which God prepared in advance for us to do' (Eph 2:10).

The church planter often believes he can do things better all by himself. In so doing, he impedes the growth of the believers. He needs to learn to look upon himself as a trainer, in order, as Paul puts it, 'to prepare God's people for works of service' (Eph 4:12).

Fear of exercising discipline

In the early stages of church planting we would prefer not to

have people leave us after just a short while. This can give rise
to the danger of a permissive attitude towards sin. We are to
sit with sinners, but when they have come to know and follow
Christ, they should embark upon a new life and abandon sinful ways. When discipline has to be exercised, there is often
hesitation because the person in question might leave, and
others as well. The tempting thought comes to us, 'We are
such a little flock, what will happen if some of us leave?' We
are called, however, to follow the biblical pattern in building
and developing the church. Paul calls us not only to build the
right foundations but to be careful as to how we build on them
(1 Cor 3:10).

The motives which drive us to practise discipline need to be
pure. The biblical purpose of discipline is to win people back
from the tyranny of sin, and return them to the Lord and His
church. We should not misuse discipline to discourage difficult people from coming, neither should we close our eyes to
sin because of personal considerations: 'We need to ask ourselves how discipline actually functions among us as Christians.'[7]

Shaky foundations

Quality must come before quantity. The church can only be
built according to the plan of Him who has bought it with His
blood. The example of Jesus in John 6 is an encouragement in
this respect. When many turned away from Him, He asked of
the twelve: 'You do not want to leave, too, do you?' (Jn 6:67)
The Lord Jesus apparently had no interest in keeping the
group large at the cost of purity. The quality of the initial
stages of church planting determines to a great extent the
future course of the church.

The church needs to be a pure instrument in the hands of
God. George B. Duncan, talking about the principle and
practice of separation from a sinful world, says that God's
people need to learn to think both in terms of separation

'from' and separation 'for': 'They are not kept sterile simply for the sake of being sterile. They are kept sterile so that they can be used.'[8] The church is the new fellowship of God's people, a holy nation belonging to God for the sake of proclaiming God's works and virtues. Therefore, we are not to make compromises and turn a blind eye to sinful lifestyles and habits. It is Christ's wish to make His church into an example for the entire world. When it is lack-lustre and has lost its Master's splendour, it will no longer reflect His image and fail to do what it is called to do.

Dead traditions

In his thesis for the Belgian Bible Institute, Andre Hofer argues that 'One of the stumbling blocks for Christian growth is tradition. Christians discover solid customs as an aid towards making their faith practical, and these solid customs soon become solid traditions—a house abandoned long ago by its inhabitants.'[9]

In many instances this leads to trouble. I recall an incident when a brother was strongly against men having beards. The obsession had taken such a hold on him that he believed beards were an Old Testament tradition, like circumcision. So why did those men with beards not let themselves be circumcised as well? He might have meant well, but in no way did it help win people for Christ, especially men with beards!

There are more subtle examples. Take raising hands while singing hymns or during prayer, for example. Up to a few years ago that was unusual. Prayers were said with closed eyes and folded hands. Today, many feel the inclination to give physical expression to their songs of praise and prayers. Andrew Kane tells of a lady who came up to him and inquired, 'I've got perfect liberty in the Lord not to raise my hands in worship, haven't I?' He answered that 'this is in fact only true if one has broken free from the tradition which says that you must not raise your hands; if you have broken free, then you are at liberty to raise your hands or not as you feel appropriate in the Spirit.'[10] More often than not we simply feel inhibited to be our own spontaneous selves in the service of the Lord. All kinds of customs and traditions have come to rule over us and curtail our freedom. We create the kind of rubble that Nehemiah found at the walls of Jerusalem, by which the rebuilding was seriously impeded.

The gravest mistake

After considering several reasons why things could go wrong and realising that the list could easily be ten times longer, we could be in danger of making the gravest mistake there is—to do nothing at all. We are imperfect people and no one knows that better than God Himself. Nevertheless, He has entrusted the gospel to us, and given us the command to make disciples of all nations. As we ponder the task of planting churches, we can say with Paul, 'Who is equal to such a task?' (2 Cor 2:16) This question calls for an answer, and the answer is this: 'Our competence comes from God' (2 Cor 3:5). This is how we should view our mission.

God will do His work through us, and when there are mistakes and shortcomings it is good to know that He uses even those to good advantage. He is building His church and we are invited to be part of it. We should not be discouraged, but be brave and get going. Just put yourself under His guidance and ask, 'Lord, where do you want me to start?'

Notes

[1]   Peter Cotterell, 'Cross-Cultural Church Planting: A Comment from the Field of Human Communications', in *How to Plant Churches* ed Monica Hill (MARC Europe: London, 1984), p 118.

[2]   Gene A. Getz, *Sharpening the Focus of the Church* (Moody Press: Chicago, 1974), p 43.

3 Robert Scott-Cook, 'The Experience of Church Planting on Large Housing Estates', in *How to Plant Churches*, p 78.

4 Melvin L. Hodge, Un guide pour l'implantation d'églises (Assemblées de Dieu: Brussels, 1977), p 54.

5 Melvin L. Hodge, *On the Mission Field: The Indigenous Church* (1953). Quoted in Burnett, in *How to Plant Churches*, p 46.

6 C. Peter Wagner, *On the Crest of the Wave: Becoming a World Christian* (Regal Books: Ventura, California, 1983), p 144.

7 Bram Krol, *Onder commando: een kompas voor de gemeente van Jezus Christus* (Telos Interlektuur: Arnhem, 1979), p 106.

8 George B. Duncan, *Pastor and People: A Devotional Commentary on II Corinthians* (Word Books: London, 1972), p 75.

9 Andre Hofer, 'Gemeente-vorming', Thesis Bijbelinstituut Belgie 1975 p 19.

10 Andrew Kane, *Let There Be Life: The Pain and Joy of Renewal in a Local Church* (Marshall Morgan & Scott: Basingstoke, 1983), pp 41–42.

PART III

9

The Continuation of the Church

I am about to tell you a sad story—hardly a pleasant thing for me to do. It is about a young couple who felt called to full-time gospel ministry. They had a vision to proclaim the good news and plant churches. When they had been trained they embarked on their mission enthusiastically. The work was hard, but they had courage and energy. They shared the gospel in many different ways. People were converted and a small fellowship was started. The work grew steadily, though not quickly.

After a few years, the fellowship could afford a small building of its own where people met for services, and youth and children's activities. Capable men were appointed as elders to carry responsibility. Our couple and their fellowship were beginning to see themselves as a church. They were respected by other churches and sometimes served as an example of how a similar venture should be managed. Eventually there were between fifty and a hundred church members.

Time went by and the church planter became the pastor rather than a pioneer evangelist. There were many things to organise and put in order. Slowly a new attitude was adopted by the fellowship and the evangelist, a self-congratulatory attitude. They felt they had arrived. They had become an established and widely respected church. The evangelist did not entertain the idea of moving on. He had invested too many years in that area; his children went to school and had friends there. They were accepted by the people around them and were on friendly terms with the mayor and other people of note, who also respected their work. In short, they had built their own little kingdom and had no intention of leaving it all behind.

By degrees, the church began to lose its vitality. There were personality clashes. Attention was focused inside; members concentrated more on each other in their observations and prayers, rather than on the lost around them. Some people left because of problems that were created. Sunday preaching lacked the fire and fervour of earlier days and there were no newcomers. When someone came in from the outside, he found it difficult to integrate. The church was a closed circle and there was little room for outsiders. Numbers slowly dropped. When someone left, an acceptable explanation was found. 'These are the last days and apostasy is bound to happen.' 'Faith will not be found with all.' These and other scriptures were quoted out of context by way of explanation, but nobody dealt with the actual causes.

It is now twenty-five or thirty years since this couple started their work, and they look back on their life's work. The church has dwindled to some fifteen members. On special Sundays there may be thirty, perhaps thirty-five. Those are high spots. The small building looks a bit run down and there is a musty smell. The fellowship has completely lost the magnetism of the early days. In a little while, there will be a funeral.

A true story? Certainly, and not the only one of its kind. This story can be retold ten or twelve times with minor differences. Some versions have a more dramatic ending, with splits leaving three tiny groups of sterile Christians claiming to have the truth and being the church of Christ in their corner of the world. I am telling this story for us to draw lessons from it. There are plenty of similar situations, and history repeats itself time and again. As Nancy and Derek Copley have pointed out, 'Since we cannot blame God for the problems in our churches, then we have to admit that they are caused by people.'[1] Many well-meaning people start with enthusiasm but have not counted the cost. They have not considered the hardships found along the way they have chosen to follow.

Many churches which remain dependent on their planter for too long appear to be particularly vulnerable to problems of the sort described above. David Burnett has observed that 'Missionary work has been aptly compared to the scaffolding used in the erection of a building. It would not speak well for the work of a builder if he had to leave the scaffolding up so that the building would not fall down!'[2] When the church remains dependent on the planter and on everything he is, does and represents, it is in a bad way. Mission researchers who have examined these problems speak of an 'effectiveness crisis' in this respect. All Christian organisations and churches run that risk.

Reasons for decline

A formerly healthy church can start declining for many reasons. When doctrine is watered down, there is often a decrease in interest as well. Where conviction is found lacking, a church loses the reason for its existence. When we set about adapting the Bible to human expectations and our much praised intellect begins to have the better of divine revelation, our church is no more than a social club with a faint Christian flavour. It has little to offer and people will lose interest.

The same holds true for pluralism. When a church condones several theologies and theories are allowed to exist alongside each other, it loses its power of attraction. At the opposite end we have legalism, with much the same effect. When the Bible and, more often, traditions are continually used to tell people what to do and what not to do, we shall drive everyone away.

A more practical reason why churches decline is failure to transfer leadership. Church planters often wish to leave their church in a near-perfect state. That is why they are late in appointing local leaders, who are then likely to be mere puppets. Working in the church planter's shadow, they have no space to develop their special gifts and skills. Peter Wagner has said that 'One of the most common ways of getting sidetracked is to fall into what I would like to call the syndrome of church development. If I were to make a catalog of missionary maladies, I would put this one high on the list.'[4]

Church development in Wagner's terms involves the desire and ambition to build the ideal church. Paul seems to have been unaffected by this desire. He taught all of God's counsel and entrusted his ministry to the Holy Spirit. In the classic he wrote about missions, Roland Allen argues that 'The first and most striking difference between his actions and ours is that he founded 'churches' whilst we found 'Missions'.'[5] Allen is saying that there is a tendency to start an organisation, part of which is the church, rather than an autonomous church which we release and leave in other hands as soon as possible. Allen observes, 'Thus St Paul seems to have left his newly-founded churches with a simple system of Gospel teaching, two sacraments, a tradition of the main facts of the death and resurrection, and the Old Testament.'[6]

Today we would probably lack the courage to plant churches in the same way. To our mind, it would be walking on thin ice. This raises the question: 'How much faith do we have in the Holy Spirit and in the work He is doing in the new converts?' Confidence in the newly converted and local leadership must be encouraged from the very start. Even when a church is started by a number of people living in the area, it will be necessary to look around for renewal and invigoration in the area of leadership. Gifts are usually developed when they are needed. Sometimes more can be achieved by stepping aside and making room for others. Leadership becomes rigid after a while and the church will need a blast of fresh air.

Keeping the vision fresh is an important element in

preventing a church from dying a slow death. We need to know whether the church is an end in itself or rather an instrument and a means of achieving God's work in the world. Eddie Gibbs is very perceptive about this:

> Despite the fact that the scriptures are so clear about what is expected of us, most churches do not work towards objectives. They lose themselves in activities. Their concern is to keep moving rather than to go anywhere. They are like a sailor who has fallen overboard. He is alone in the water and out of sight of land. He doesn't know which way to swim, so he treads water. He knows that the moment he stops he will go down.[7]

Many churches are trapped in a round of activities. There is a routine for each week, month and year. Attention is directed inwards, instead of towards the original mission. When a fellowship is introspective and programme-oriented, then squabbles, frictions, self-sufficiency and other carnal conditions will often follow. People get disenchanted with each other and there are no new challenges to stimulate us to prayer and action. When we cannot fight together against the Enemy who attacks from without, hostility will grow within us. There will be spiritual lukewarmness in the church, and that is disastrous in the long term.

God makes us partakers of His salvation so that we might become sharers. We shall discuss the church and its mission, locally and internationally, in the next chapter. The issue is not only that the gospel is spread by means of the local church. For its own survival the church needs to be intensely occupied with that mission. Jesus taught that the vine has branches so that it can bear fruit. When it bears no fruit, the branches are cut off and thrown into the fire (Jn 15:2,6). In this context, we could refer to the letters to the seven churches in Revelation chapters 2 and 3.

Another reason why a church may relapse is if Jesus Christ is no longer centre stage. In the letters to the seven churches, Christ is called the One who 'walks among the seven golden lampstands' (Rev 2:1). He is the Head of the universal church and the leader of all local churches. At least, He is supposed to be that. In one of his sermons, A. W. Tozer says, 'Blessed is the church which has Jesus Christ as its one single attraction.' He is the One who assures access to the Father, and as His church we are the instrument by which He wants to be active in the world. Our Lord is the Head, and we need to listen to Him and do as He commands us, in obedience to Him. The question again is: 'Have we learned to listen to Him? Do we experience His leading?' This is one of the signs which show whether the church is alive. When as His church we do not recognise His voice, do not act upon it, there will be signs of paralysis. Roland Allen writes:

> The reason of our failure is, I believe, largely due to the fact that we quench that Spirit. We educate our converts to think, as we, accustomed to a long-established and highly-organized church, naturally think, that none but duly appointed ministers may preach. We dread the possible mistakes of individual zeal. The result is that our converts hesitate to speak of religion to others. They throw the responsibility upon the licensed evangelist and 'the mission.' They do not feel any responsibility themselves to evangelize the world. Their mouths are closed. Here and there, of course, we find a man so full of the Spirit of the Lord that he cannot hold his peace, but he is a comparatively rare exception.[8]

God's work in the world

Jesus Christ is actively involved in everything He means to do through His church, but not necessarily in everything the church does. When Paul persecuted the early church with the express intention of destroying it, the risen Lord called a halt and cried out to him, 'Saul, Saul, why do you persecute me?' (Acts 9:4). This gives us something to think about. Paul persecuted the disciples, yet Jesus said, 'Why do you persecute me?' Jesus is much more closely involved with the church than we usually think. He is active in the world through His church.

Therefore, when a church listens to Him carefully and follows His instructions, what that church does must have a greater impact for eternity than any human endeavour. Christians, resolved to follow Him, have more effect than the United Nations or the government of a particular country. Jesus stated that the disciples' mission did not differ in principle or method from His own. He started by granting them His authority and power to do His work (Mk 6:7; Mt 10:1; Lk 9:1), and finished by telling them to do it as He Himself would. Coleman exclaims, 'Think of this identity!' when he quotes Jesus' words: 'He who receives you receives me, and he who receives me receives the one who sent me' (Mt 10:40; Jn 13:20).[9] Everyday living is no different; we are to do as Christ would in everyday living as well.

I am reminded of a 'tough guy' in Brussels—one of the many there—who was confronted with the gospel of Jesus Christ. God spoke to him and he was saved by grace and the love of God. Christ's blood washed away all his sins and he began life afresh immediately. That was not easy, since up to that point he had stolen motor bikes and cars for a living. Without going into details which would reveal his identity, today he owns a garage and has become a dependable man. Everyone he meets knows him to be honest. Recently a client wrote him a letter expressing his appreciation for his skill and honesty. There is only one other Christian in his family, but his testimony has made an impression. They are puzzled about what has happened. Spiritual strength makes such a powerful impact![10]

In this way, Jesus is still making lives new. The church is in the world as Jesus was in it—in the world, but not of it. We represent God's new order. The church is a sign and symbol of the new fellowship, the glorious kingdom of God of which Christ is Lord. That is why the function of the church is to be light and salt in today's world, a society that is rot-proof, moth-proof and stainless. Reporting his evangelistic activities, Bruno Herm recounts a visit to the Solomon Islands:

Where churches are planted, we see social changes. I am
reminded of a visit to sister Leonide Grauman on the Solomon
Islands. I had my luggage, camera and everything else a person
has to watch closely when visiting Asia in the car and when I got
out of it, I was preparing to lock it. She, on the other hand, left the
window open in her own car, closed the door and said, 'A few days
ago, I left my wallet on the car seat by accident. Although the window was open, it was still there when I came back to it. Churches
are leaving their mark everywhere in the country; the impact of
the gospel can be seen wherever you go.' [11]

That is how it was where Jesus passed, when He walked the
earth. The unclean became clean where He went. His presence had a sanctifying impact, not so much because he put
right all kinds of situations, but because, before all else, He
was dedicated to God. And that made all things new. Simi-
larly, the church provides the link between God and this
world. The church is God's own temple. God lives in our
midst, in this world, by means of His church in which He is
present by His Spirit.

When we learn to look at the church in this way, we avoid
rigidity. We do not want to look back all the time at the progress we have made, for that is past glory already. On the contrary, we want to look towards the future. Jesus entrusts us
with new missions, new challenges are put before us. We will
need His help and grace in this area. We are not able to
achieve anything by ourselves and in our own strength. We
are continually dependent on Him. We need Him and cannot
live or accomplish our mission without Him. That is what con-
stitutes the life of the church. Being weak, we are strong.
Being fearful, we are full of courage. Being small, we are
great. In this way 'we who are alive are always being given
over to death for Jesus' sake, so that his life may be revealed in
our mortal body' (2 Cor 4:11). In the process we shall also give
new life to a world that believes it is alive but, in actual fact, is
dead. These are the principles of the kingdom of God, the

foundations upon which the life of Jesus was built.

Being attractive

As the church is so intimately united with Christ, we can learn from looking at His life how to keep the church fresh and attractive. When Christ walked this earth, people flocked to Him. They searched Him out. Children felt safe with Him, He was their friend. Sinners visited Him. Zaccheus climbed a tree to make sure he did not miss Him. The charisma that Jesus emanated needs to be felt in the church as well. Snyder has observed:

> But the church is to know the mind of Christ, the renewed image of God. In a technological age, this is revolutionary. . . . The character of Jesus Christ is the standard for the church, and there is a unique feature of Christ's character—what Paul here calls 'mind'—which the community of God's people is to experience.[12]

Endless books could be written about the qualities of Christ which made Him so attractive, qualities which should also be seen in a church that is alive and Spirit-filled. I shall limit myself to three observations.

1. Authority in love

This is the first quality which attracted people so strongly to Jesus. We find it expressed in John 1:14. The Word that 'became flesh and lived for a while among us' is said to be 'full of grace and truth.' That is an interesting combination. Jesus attracted sinners not because He excused sin and advocated mercy. On the contrary, in His eyes, sin was sin, a serious offence. It issued from the destructive desire of the human heart to rebel against its Creator. He showed just how serious this was. But when sin was named and recognised, a solution was readily at hand. When we lift a stone, we expose insects trying to hide from the full light of day. So it was with Christ.

He spoke the truth and exposed falsehood and deceit.

He spoke, however, in the spirit of love. He was full of grace and truth. The two were inextricably interwoven. Where sin was discovered and came to light, grace shone all the more brilliantly. In this way hope, salvation and deliverance were achieved. The power of renewal did not issue from compromise but rather from truth producing grace. Many people were enslaved and weighed down by the bondage of sin, continuing to sin in an attempt to cover up previous sins. God's grace came like a revolution into their lives.

In John 8:7–11 we find a practical example: a woman caught in the act of adultery is brought before Jesus. What is to happen to her? Judgement of sin and the practice of love appear to be on a collision course. In a wonderful way Jesus solves this: 'If anyone of you is without sin, let him be the first to throw a stone at her.' When the accusers have left one by one, Jesus asks, '"Has no one condemned you?" "No one, sir," she said. "Then neither do I condemn you," Jesus declared. "Go now and leave your life of sin".' That was the crucial point: sin was recognised as sin, and the truth was told. But grace provided the solution, 'go and sin no more,' and forgiveness was given.

This authority in love reflected Jesus' relationship with His Father. People tasted God in what Jesus said and did. He was God incarnate and was recognised as such. In the same way, we shall be recognised as a church. We too are able to live in relationship with the heavenly Father and learn to do as He says. This enables us to reflect God's truth and grace:

> So authority generally, and God's authority in particular, is the central issue of the universe and certainly the central issue of any biblical church community. . . . That is what the kingdom implies: it is God's reign, God's rule, God's control, God's government of our lives.[13]

This is what we need to learn as a church. This is our high

calling. The closer we draw to God—the more carefully we listen to His voice and do as He bids us—the more we shall resemble Him and pass on His grace and truth. Snyder reminds us that 'Believers need to know by experience that the Most High God is also the Most Nigh God (Is. 57:15).'[14] That is grace and truth. When the church is filled with it, it will go out into the world as a servant. It will be attractive because Christ will be recognised through it.

2. Inner harmony

This is the second quality which made Jesus so attractive. He was so at one with Himself! Peace went with Him wherever He went. The women who were delivered through His ministry served Him. Children obviously felt at home with Him. His disciples experienced His inner peace and harmony in the midst of their disputes with each other. He was dragged into their discussions: 'Tell my brother to divide the inheritance with me' (Lk 12:13). There were theological disputes: 'Is there or is there not a resurrection?' (Lk 20:27). And squabbles about practical things like 'Is it right to do good on the Sabbath?' (Lk 13:15). On top of that, He was very busy. There were always people who claimed His attention. They thronged around Him and yet 'He always walked; He never ran.'[15] It was a reflection of his poise. He was in perfect harmony with God and Himself. Just like a guitar that has different strings, each string having a different sound, in the same way Christ was perfectly tuned to all situations at all times. That explains why peace filled Him to overflowing.

The church needs to be just like this: at peace with the Lord and therefore in harmony with its Creator and all men. The peace that fills us to overflowing must be seen, whatever conflicts might arise. Paul addressed the church at Philippi saying, 'Your attitude should be the same as that of Christ Jesus' (Phil 2:5). Jesus was not concerned about winning the dispute, and He did not defend His rights. He followed the narrow path of God's plan with His whole heart. He won by losing—so Philippians 2 teaches us. That is why Paul asks on a different occasion, 'Why not rather be wronged?' (1 Cor 6:7).

When this inner harmony reigns in the church, it will attract people because it makes them think of Christ. The last will come first, the small will be great and the servant a leader. The spirit of competition which fills the world will leave the church, and the church will be a place of rest from the tribulations of this world. Then the church will have a future and live up to its high calling.

3. Compassion

Compassion is another quality which made Christ attractive. The very fact that He came into the world speaks of His sympathy and compassion. He did not come for purposes of His own, but for us. His entire life was representative of this sense of compassion. He was interested in the whole person. He clearly taught that sin is the root of all sorrow, but He did not only forgive sins: He cleansed lepers, healed the sick, fed the hungry and delivered people from bondage. Peter sums up Jesus' ministry in the following terms in his address at Cornelius' house: 'he went around doing good and healing all who were under the power of the devil, because God was with him' (Acts 10:38).

Jesus saw two pictures in us. First he saw, through all pain and degeneration, God's creative purpose, a purpose for all time. He saw the original plan; that is why he preached time and again that 'The kingdom of God is near' (Mk 1:15). He said, 'This creation belongs to God and the devil has no claim on it. He is a usurper—a liar, a thief and a murderer.' Jesus was able to see the true potential of creation and man in particular. The second picture Jesus saw was the actual state of affairs, 'they were harassed and helpless' (Mt 9:36). He saw people suffer and a creation 'groaning as in the pains of childbirth' (Rom 8:22). He saw degeneration, envy, resentment and affliction. The gap between these two pictures, between what was meant to be and what was, must have caused unspeakable hurt. Jesus had compassion on the world, and this was at the centre of His relationship with it. Moved by love and compassion He accomplished His saving work for us.

The church of Christ is to look upon the world in the same way. We believe creation to be God's work and not an accidental combination of atoms. We know God's original intent for all times. We also see before us the reality of life in the world today. The gap is heart-rending and should fill our hearts with compassion. In response, we should consider the suffering of all creation, but especially that of those around us. When we meet people bound by sin, ravaged by illness, struck down by disappointment, our heart should break when we think of how life could have been. When we see people bogged down in sin, we need to pass on God's scheme of redemption. Whenever people suffer, we need to pray with and for them, and help them. The compassion of Christ needs to take shape in our lives. When this becomes a reality, the church will flourish and fulfil its divine intentions, for it will then resemble Christ, and that is the best way of ensuring that Christ's church does not go into decline.

The secret of Jesus' attractiveness was:

1   Authority in love: His relationship with the Father.
    Where does our church stand in this?
2   Inner harmony: His relationship with Himself.
    Where does our church stand in this?
3   Compassion for the whole person: His relationship with the world.
    Where does our church stand in this?

I started this chapter on a sad note, but it need not end that way. When we heed the voice of the Head of the church and put ourselves under His authority in complete obedience, a wonderful future lies ahead of us and churches will no longer fade away.

Notes

1. Derek and Nancy Copley, *Building with Bananas: People Problems in the Church* (Paternoster Press: Exeter, 1984), p 21.
2. David Burnett, in *How to Plant Churches* ed Monica Hill (MARC Europe: London, 1984), p 51.
3. James F. Engel and Wilbert Norton, *What's Gone Wrong with the Harvest?* (Zondervan: Grand Rapids, Michigan, 1982), p 20.
4. C. Peter Wagner, *On the Crest of the Wave: Becoming a World Christian* (Regal Books: Ventura, California, 1983), p 147.
5. Roland Allen, *Missionary Methods: St. Paul's or Ours?* (William B. Eerdmans: Grand Rapids, Michigan, 1979), p 83.
6. *ibid,* p 90.
7. Eddie Gibbs, *Body Building Exercises for the Local Church* (Falcon: London, 1979), p 73.
8. Allen, *op cit*, pp 93–94.
9. Robert E. Coleman, *The Master Plan of Evangelism* (Fleming H. Revell: Old Tappan, New Jersey, 1982), p 88.
10. Johan Lukasse, 'Dingen die God doet', *Evangeliekoerier* (June 1986): p 3. *Evangeliekoerier* is a bimonthly magazine issued by the Belgian Evangelical Mission at Brussels.
11. Bruno Herm, 'Wereldwijde groei van de gemeente van JEZUS', *EZA-Informatie* (April 1986): pp 12–13. *EZA-Informatie* is a trimonthly magazine issued by the Evangelical Mission Alliance Foundation (Stichting Evangelische Zendings Alliantie) at Nunspeet, The Netherlands.
12. Howard A. Snyder, *The Problem of Wineskins: Church Structures in a Technological Age* (Inter-Varsity Press: Downers Grove, Illinois, 1976), p 113.
13. Ron Trudinger, *Built to Last: Biblical Principles for Church Restoration* (Kingsway Publications: Eastbourne, 1982), pp 44–45.
14. Snyder, *op cit,* p 97.
15. Engel and Norton, *op cit,* p 107.

10

The Church and its Mission

How can we reach nominal Christians with the gospel? Large numbers of people still call themselves Christians. They have some link with a church, but in their church there is no trace of real spiritual life. Traditional rituals are maintained, and some kind of social activity continues, but the message is watered down and without power. Such a church is no more than an empty shell, a spiritual graveyard. People attend these churches but remain ignorant of God and His truth. They constitute a mission field.

This problem has given rise to a great deal of discussion. Do we co-operate with these churches and bring the gospel to their flock with their leaders' consent? Or would it be more fruitful to reach nominal Christians individually? Should we simply ignore their links with a watered-down, tradition-bound church? Several evangelistic movements of an inter-denominational nature have chosen to work with this type of church. They aim to evangelise from within. The problem is then: Where should people go for further instruction after they have accepted Christ? Should they stay in their dead churches? House groups are often seen as the solution, but if the converts maintain their links with the traditional church they are not able to develop into new churches.

This brings us back to some of the questions we dealt with in Chapter 3. Do we need to stay with these churches, or part company? Some will argue that many more people can be reached by evangelising from within. There are fewer prejudices to be overcome and we are able to approach people in a more normal and acceptable way. Others argue differently. According to Pierre Wheeler:

> . . . it is more or less saying to the new babe in Christ—we can give you your bottles, but as for your future home, it's a question of 'getting on as best you can.' It is not just the utensils he's lacking . . . the babe just has no home and will be raised in the street. This is surely unbiblical.[1]

Born in the street

In the New Testament the proclamation of the gospel was the responsibility of the local church. Acts 13 tells us that the local church launched evangelistic effort. Next we see that the activities of the early missionaries led to the planting of new local churches. It could be argued that there were no lukewarm or dead churches at that time. On the other hand, Paul never left his disciples behind in the synagogue. He planted new churches in very difficult and risky circumstances. Often leaders were appointed only on the return journey, when the apostle visited a second time.

On Paul's second missionary journey this is even more obvious. In Acts 17:4 we read that people not only were persuaded and believed, but also joined Paul and Silas. This small group grew to be a church. The individual spiritual maturity of every member was a sure sign of being part of a church. Every member understood the necessity of helping each other grow in faith, knowledge and understanding, as well as in living out the Christian life.

In Chapter 1 we have already explained that fellowship is a vital component of a church and is necessary for balanced growth. There is an undeniable link between individual growth and the growth in numbers of believers. The first few lines of the letters to the Corinthians, Philippians and Thessalonians were addressed to established churches. That is far more significant than would appear at first sight. Good churches are necessary for the 'continuation of the species'. When children are born into good families, not on the streets, they stand a good chance of developing into balanced personalities who, in their turn, can build normal families. The church is not an end in itself. It is God's instrument by which His message can be proclaimed throughout the world.

God's plan

When Jesus Christ, our risen Lord, sent out His disciples, He said, 'Therefore, go and make disciples of all nations' (Mt 28:19). This was the mission He entrusted to us, to go and make disciples. Earlier, He had told them, 'I will build my church' (Mt 16:18). This was His promise to us. Until Jesus returns we have His mission to fulfil and His promise to reassure us. Everybody should have the opportunity to turn to God and belong to Him again. That has become possible ever since Christ rose from the dead and cleared the way for us to live in harmony with our Creator. There is forgiveness of sins for everyone. We start life afresh with the coming of the Holy Spirit. All of this is entirely free and available to every one who puts his trust in God and believes that Christ's death on the cross took away his sins. Acts 2:11 shows us that this message was not proclaimed to the world by the apostles alone, but by the whole church. The church is an instrument in God's hand. It takes the powers of hell by surprise. It reveals God's wisdom for all to see (Eph 3:10).

What are God's intentions for the church? In the first place, it is there to glorify God in praise and adoration. It acknowledges Him as sovereign on His throne and ruler of the universe. There is still that dark and usurping power which brings affliction and decay into this world. But Jesus said after He rose from the dead, 'All authority in heaven and on earth has been given to me' (Mt 28:18). His church recognises His dominion. It glorifies God by listening to His voice and living in a new Scripture-based obedience, in honour of His name.

The second reason for the existence of the church is to proclaim the message of God. Peter said:

> But you are a chosen people, a royal priesthood, a holy nation, a people belonging to God, that you may declare the praises of him who called you out of darkness into his wonderful light. Once you were not a people, but now you are the people of God; once you had not received mercy, but now you have received mercy (1 Pet 2:9–10).

So we have been chosen for a purpose, in order to complete a task. Having tasted salvation, you are privileged to tell others about God's greatness.

In describing our calling to declare God's praises, Peter uses the Greek word that can be translated 'virtues' as well as 'deeds'. I take it to mean that we have been chosen to proclaim the mighty deeds that issue from God's virtues. It was God's love that Jesus revealed, and God's power that raised Him from the dead. The church has the privilege of being a messenger of this. It has the special right to tell people who God really is and what He has done for us and all creation.

The story is told of Jesus arriving back in heaven. The angels asked, 'Will you let us proclaim the good news to the world?' He answered, 'No, I will not. The only people who can pass on the good news are those who have experienced it. Salvation will be preached by saved sinners and no one else.' That is precisely what the church has been chosen to do.

The third reason for the church's existence is that by its mediation God is present in this world. God lives among His people. In the Old Testament this was effected by the altar and the Temple. In His farewell Jesus promised not to leave His disciples behind as orphans. He would return and live among them (Jn 14:15–18). In his first letter to the Corinthians, Paul refers to the church as 'God's temple' (3:16). Some people believe that the universal church (which is invisible) is meant. Michael Griffiths refutes this:

> The late Allan Stibbs had an apt illustration of this double use in which he would point out that we use the one expression 'the moon' whether we are viewing the full moon, the half moon or even the slenderest of crescent moons.[3]

The church of Jesus Christ becomes visible in the local church. Although it is larger than is obvious at a particular time and location, it still finds its expression in the local church. In this way God has purposed to be in the world through His church. That includes the local church, His visible representative, which is an immensely high calling and privilege. This is what Paul wants to impress upon the believers at Ephesus:

> His intent was that now, through the church, the manifold wisdom of God should be made known to the rulers and authorities in the heavenly realms, according to his eternal purpose which he accomplished in Christ Jesus our Lord. In him and through faith in him we may approach God with freedom and confidence (Eph 3:10–12).

Keeping the entire church of Christ in view is therefore of the utmost importance. When we learn to see the grandeur of God's plan for the church, we shall begin to understand its task and mission. Terry Virgo has put it this way:

> God often asks the prophets 'What do you see?' What you will see will determine what you build. . . . When the vision of the Kingdom of God fills our horizon, it will affect our whole lifestyle, our values and our decisions.[4]

River or reservoir?

Once we have understood God's purpose for the church and have brought our expectations in line with it, we have a magnificent goal in life. We begin to understand that we do not 'arrive' the moment we become Christians and join a church—that is only the starting-point! Nothing equals the challenge to join others in being God's instrument in this world.

Think of the lake of Galilee: fresh and living water pours into it, and leaves it at the other end. The lake is filled with fish and other living creatures. Further on, however, this same water ends up in the Dead Sea where it has no exit to flow away. As the name indicates, there is no life in that stretch of water. Birds steer clear of it and there is hardly any vegetation alongside the shore.

The same principle applies to local churches. When they exist only by receiving they are utterly unattractive and will die a quick death. When individual Christians join a church because they want to receive something, they will soon notice that something is missing. When, on the other hand, they show that they want to contribute positively to God's plan and purpose, they will receive a great deal. This attitude is important both individually and collectively. A life of giving, sharing and receiving is what God has in mind for us. There needs to be a desire to serve and accomplish God's plan, and then to be replenished by fellowship with others, continuing the work of God. When we give away what we have, we shall become spiritually hungry again.

This is apparent in many practical ways. A Belgian brother once told me how he recovered from discouragement. 'It's very simple,' he replied, smiling. 'I had to lead a Bible study on Saturday night and needed to prepare for it. I felt completely empty spiritually but I started anyway. As I progressed and studied the passage more closely, my joy slowly came back. At last, I was so charged up that I could hardly wait to pass on what had been given to me. When I began to speak, I felt really happy and my depression had left me.' As he was telling the story, the words of Moses came to me, 'I wish that all the Lord's people were prophets' (Num 11:29).

For some years I have been actively involved with evangelistic campaigns. Time and again I have witnessed their effect on believers. People were sent out to proclaim the gospel, the majority of them with shaking knees. The praying that followed was more intense than usual. 'Help me, God, I can't do it!' God answers this kind of prayer, and their life of faith became fresh and new once more.

Soon they realised that people were not exactly eager to hear what Christians had to say about their faith. Hard questions were levelled at them which they had to answer. Together they had to formulate an answer and in this way became more eager to receive further instruction themselves. They learned things extra fast! They felt the need of it. Teaching answered a felt need and the questions they asked related to their own experience. When the teaching did not entirely settle the problem at hand, teachers would be informed of this instantly! So the teachers were stimulated, in their turn, and the quality of their teaching improved. Believers were melted together into a church as they went into battle together. Each member needed the other and minor differences which otherwise took much time and attention, disappeared as snow before the sun.

I am convinced that this is the only way to stay alive as a church: always to pass on what we believe and why we believe. In so doing we provide the opportunity for others to be saved by the power and grace of God. S. D. Gordon has argued that:

> The church or the man that selfishly saves his life shall lose it. He that forgets about his own life in eagerly saving others shall find that he has saved his own life, and that it has grown into a new fullness and richness.[5]

This is the very spirit of the gospel. God's word will be of value to us only as we pass it on to others. It will grow richer as we give it away. It will be rooted more firmly in our hearts, the more often we help others to it. Living through giving will be our experience as we follow in our Master's footsteps.

Jerusalem first

The task of sharing starts right on your own doorstep. When Jesus gave the Great Commission, He suggested a definite order of precedence: 'But you will receive power when the Holy Spirit comes on you; and you will be my witnesses in Jerusalem, and in all Judea and Samaria, and to the ends of the earth' (Acts 1:8). The disciples were in Jerusalem at the time. That was the immediate environment and that was where they had to start as soon as the Holy Spirit descended on them. The age of the church was heralded in. A few weeks after Pentecost, Jerusalem was 'filled' with their teaching (Acts 5:28).

This procedure is still valid today. The church is there to witness first of all in its local environment. It is to radiate the gospel. In some churches people understand this and want to evangelise, but are uncertain as to how to get started. Possibly this idea might help. Every church member could make a list of five people he knows and to whom he would like the gospel explained. The list is a reminder to pray for these people daily. Another church member could join him to pray for the people on the list.

In this way we could encourage one another, asking questions and offering suggestions, being faithful in prayer and then approaching these people at the right time. We could assist each other by discussing the appropriate approach. Our personal witness is boosted and, if need be, corrected by others. When there is progress, there will be general rejoicing. We need to make a start with what we should like to happen; most of us do not even reach that point.

I have seen this method operate in various situations. When people are converted, we move their names on to a new column on the list, entitled 'Growth towards Spiritual Maturity'.

We then tell people that the list has had their names on it for some time now, and that the time has come for them to draw up a list of their own of people with whom they would like to share this good news. We will make it our business to direct and assist them. In this way we do not just win people, we train soul-winners as well. John Bisagno has given a useful definition:

> What is evangelism? Evangelism is that complete process by which the evangelized themselves become evangelists. In other words, merely winning men to Christ is not the end of our job. It is but the beginning. The process of evangelism includes making converts of sinners, disciples of converts, and soul-winners of disciples.[6]

As can be expected, enthusiasm plays an important role. It is a great energiser and makes witnessing much easier, 'For out of the overflow of the heart the mouth speaks' (Mt 12:34). Enthusiasm motivates people and this involves a lot more than a passing show of emotion. Bisagno reminds us that 'the very word "enthuse" comes from two Greek words "en" and "theos." It means simply "in God" and "God in you." "God in you" carries the picture of the lesser containing the greater.'[7] It is God's Spirit working in us. The disciples needed the power of God's Spirit to be active through them. It is precisely this presence of the Spirit of God which makes a real church. We should beware of reducing the witness of the church to speaking about Christ and His mission. The church needs to embody Christ in spirit and in action. There are many outside who are hurting, in distress and need. The church needs to learn how to recognise them and minister to them in the power of God, offering comfort to hurt emotions and living proof of divine love.

The church should hold on to the vision for church planting, and become the instrument for planting new churches in its area. It should prosper by division. When this happens in a spirit of prayer, it will be in accord with the command God gave to His church and provide a rich blessing. Andrew Kane has observed that 'These churches had grown by sending out members to plant churches. This always led to further growth.'[8]

The next stage

The church's mission starts close to home, but does not stop there. The next step Jesus commanded involved Judea and Samaria. This was neighbouring territory. It was not the city or the suburbs, but distant country. You could compare it with the provinces of your own country, or even neighbouring countries. Samaria was a region with a foreign population. How that came to be is told in 2 Kings 17:24–41. Moreover, a mixture of religions had intermingled with the faith of Israel. That explains Jewish disgust with everything Samaritan. Jesus told the disciples to go there as well, in His power. In the same way we need to go to the many foreigners in our cities.

It is a difficult step, since we meet all kinds of religions and cultures. The church at Jerusalem did not take this step at first. God needed to send persecution their way before they got started. It was not until Stephen was stoned to death and the disciples were scattered throughout Judea and Samaria, that they 'preached the word wherever they went' (Acts 8:1,4). Only then did the message of salvation reach Samaria and Antioch.

The church at Antioch consisted almost entirely of Gentiles and provided the impetus for the evangelistic journeys of Paul and his team. Churches must be involved in proclaiming the good news, even if they cannot necessarily expect their church to grow in numbers as a result. Their world mission is to work for the well-being of others in a disinterested way. In imitation of Christ's coming down from His heavenly glory to a world estranged from God, the church is called and privileged to do the same in His name.

Today a wide range of tools is at our disposal to assist us in executing this part of our mission. Evangelistic campaigns need to be organised and executed by all the manpower we can get. The churches would do well to look at mission fields which are close to home. There are large numbers of foreigners in our cities and the organisations working for them need our help.

Take the Muslims, for example. Many Christians shrink from approaching them with the good news. What are we afraid of? Do we not know how, or is it that we would rather not? Will God have to allow another persecution to happen before the church performs this task? Churches that support mission close to home have been blessed. Every act of obedience to God is enriching. I have seen Christians from England and the Netherlands contribute to the Belgian campaigns and be of great help; they have been refreshed and blessed in the process. There are similar examples of Germans helping on Austrian campaigns, and Scandinavians assisting in Spain and Italy. Short-term missions are executed by American teams in certain parts of Europe with much blessing from the Lord.

It is of vital importance that the entire church gets involved in the campaign. Even if some are unable to participate, they can be involved in prayer or in practical preparations and, occasionally, home assignments. Others will help later with follow-up work. Reporting back to the sending churches is very valuable at this stage, as workers share what the Lord has accomplished and give Him the honour in thanksgiving and worship. This is an uplifting experience for the church that has offered its people to help.

Unto the ends of the earth

The commission in Acts 1:8 makes it clear that the disciples could not choose between being witnesses in Jerusalem or Judea and Samaria, or the ends of the earth. They were not asked to choose between one mission field or another. The church in its turn is responsible for passing on the gospel to the ends of the earth, starting close to home. Our standard reaction to this is, 'But that cannot be done!' But would God ask us to do something we are unable to do in His power? This is the ultimate test of our faith and obedience. We need to start in all simplicity where we are and turn what we have to good use.

When the church at Antioch was fasting and praying together, the Holy Spirit spoke and gave the commission for appointing the first missionaries. Humanly speaking, it could not be predicted at that time that by this effort all of Asia Minor and part of Europe would hear God's message in the space of a single generation.

Through fasting and prayer we must ask God how He wishes us to accomplish our mission. We could, for example, appoint a church member to pass on information about world evangelism. As the number of believers increases we might soon have a full-fledged missionary task force. Every Sunday attention could be directed to a particular country and its special needs, and we could pray for it. In this way, we could encourage our people to become 'world Christians'. A world Christian is not to be confused with a worldly Christian. In *In the Gap,* David Bryant depicts the world Christian with a few firm brushstrokes: 'World Christians are day-to-day disciples for whom Christ's global cause has become the integrating, overriding priority for all that He is for them.'[9]

However small a church might be, it can make a start on the Great Commission. In co-operation with a larger church in the area a mission conference could be organised and the growing church could receive a broader vision and begin to bear responsibility for worldwide evangelism.

At a later stage this could result in God calling certain individuals in the church to the mission field. The identification of this calling is then the responsibility of the church as a whole and not just the individual Christian. When the Holy Spirit at Antioch set apart for Himself the first missionaries, He chose people who were already actively serving the Lord. Later on, He set them apart in two different stages: in the first place, with the leaders as they were actively serving the Lord; in the second place, the church prayed and fasted, before they let them go (Acts 13:1–3). The calling was recognised and confirmed by the whole church.

Many missionary organisations are confronted with the question of how to select their missionary candidates effectively. When the vision and calling are born in the local church, it is able to discern whether this calling is from God. The local leaders and the entire fellowship will deflate the balloon in no time should it be no more than a passing impulse. However, when someone is already occupied in his own church with winning others for Christ and shows compassion for those that are lost, his calling will soon be recognised as authentic. In Gene Getz's opinion, 'the church is responsible to identify those who feel especially called by God to carry the good news in a special way out into the community and beyond the immediate community—even to 'the remotest parts of the earth.'[10] The church is responsible for this identification, and not a missionary organisation, even though at a later stage the co-operation, experience and specialised assistance of such an organisation would be required in order to prepare the way. The observations below might help to keep in clear view the Great Commission and put it into practice.

1 Acquiring love for missionary work

This seems to be a good starting-point. It is where the mission of Jesus Christ started and where ours needs to start as well. At the centre there is love for God and His creation, and especially for people in places where the gospel has never been told. Information is of tantamount importance here. It is hard to love what we do not know. The information stage can start early. Many missionaries claim to have received their first calling at Sunday school, before they were ten years old. That first calling recedes into the background for a while and then comes back. We need to instil in church members a love for missionaries. It is much easier to love missionaries than to love an organisation. Reports need to be shared with the church, sermon illustrations taken from information about missionaries. This will give us a vision and love for the work that is so close to God's heart. When we love what He loves we are on the right track.

2 Praying for the mission

This is a very direct way of being involved. I know a congregation which as a rule prays every Sunday for a missionary far away. People are told where they work and how they are doing. Blessings and needs are passed on and a time of prayer follows. The church is encouraged to pray for that particular person or that family in the week ahead. When prayers are answered, this is communicated in church and the bond of love grows stronger. This again stimulates the desire to be a part of the last command Christ gave us before He went back to heaven.

3 Financial support

Giving financially is a great opportunity for the church to show that it takes the Great Commission seriously. In the context of gospel proclamation, money is often a delicate subject. We seem to need time to become persuaded that 'It is more blessed to give than to receive' (Acts 20:35). Missionaries find it difficult to explain that money is necessary for their work to go on: 'Surveys have shown that one of the most distasteful aspects of missionary service, particularly for young people today, is fund raising. I call it the "tin-cup complex."'[11]

Nevertheless, the Bible associates great blessings with generous giving. The example of Jesus Christ Himself is put before us: 'For you know the grace of our Lord Jesus Christ, that though he was rich, yet for your sakes he became poor, so that you through his poverty might become rich' (2 Cor 8:9). What a blessing we could be as a church by taking on a clearly defined responsibility for supporting missionaries. Our example will often encourage other churches to give similar support. Taking to heart the teachings of the Bible, together we can put into practice what Jesus said about looking for the right treasures: 'Do not store up for yourselves treasures on earth, where moth and rust destroy, and where thieves break in and steal. But store up for yourselves treasures in heaven, where moth and rust do not destroy, and where thieves do not break in and steal' (Mt 6:19–20). We must learn to recognise a good investment.

4 Reporting back from the mission field

Field reports to the home church help to build up a vision for missions. People want to know what is done with their support, and how their efforts contribute to the final goal through the work of others. In the first place, feed-back is the responsibility of those sent out. The home church, on the other hand, can do much to make known this valuable information. Writing to missionaries is a boost for them as they realise their letters are given attention. Photographs, audio-cassettes and newsletters can be of great service. I know some churches that send off tapes every month with recordings of services, or a newsletter, or birthday greetings. There are plenty of possibilities to develop.

5 Developing a worldwide mission information network

Another powerful strategy which could assist in gaining understanding of initiatives started in obedience to the Great Commission is the development of a worldwide information network concerning missionary work. Some organisations are already ministering to us in that way. Patrick Johnstone's *Operation World* can be of great service in this area.[12] Some churches, by means of this book, keep the whole world regularly in their prayers. When the church hears what God is doing in other parts of the world, there is a strong incentive to pray, especially when things look bad in the immediate environment. A window then opens for us on the world, disclosing God's works in this age. Church leaders should especially direct their efforts towards a world-view, broadening their field of vision. This will bless us both at home and abroad.

Working together

The observations I have just given could create the impression that local churches everywhere are expected to act upon the Great Commission on their own, without the need for missionary organisations. That is not my intention. Even in New Testament times certain people were set apart for a special mission; they were sent out. History shows that several missionary societies did work of great merit which most probably could not have been done by the local churches. Within the Roman Catholic Church, missionary work was the task of religious orders.

In the complex world of today much specialised knowledge is required to find the way through administrative red tape, before evangelists are allowed to go to another country. Upon arrival they are faced with the problem of how their home country can take care of them. New questions are added every minute, as every country is different. This state of affairs justifies the existence of missionary societies. In other words, churches cannot dodge their responsibilities and missionary societies cannot assume full responsibility. They need to work in a spirit of co-operation.

We should always strive to reach the ultimate goal of missions, the planting of new churches which, in their turn, could take over and further develop the work. There needs to be a strong foundation and a clearly outlined biblical goal. Our mission is simply too urgent; we cannot afford to be divided on the basis of smaller interests. We need to reach this generation and future ones with the message of salvation through Jesus Christ alone. Therefore, we simply cannot afford to 'play church' and run around in the same little circles for ever. There is an all-important mission to be accomplished and we need to get going, claiming the strength or *dunamis* that Christ has promised.

Notes

1 Pierre Wheeler, 'More Evangelism in Europe', in *Trinity World Forum* (Spring 1987): pp 3–4. *Trinity World Forum* is a periodical issued quarterly by the Trinity Evangelical Divinity School, Deerfield, Illinois.

2 Robert E. Coleman, *The Master Plan of Evangelism* (Fleming H. Revell: Old Tappan, New Jersey, 1982),, pp 4, 34.

3 Michael Griffiths, *Cinderella with Amnesia: A Practical Discussion of the Relevance of the Church* (Inter-Varsity Press: London, 1975), p 16.

4 Terry Virgo, *Restoration in the Church* (Kingsway Publications: Eastbourne, 1985), p 112.

5 S. D. Gordon, *What It Will Take to Change the World*, ed Dick Eastman (Baker Book House: Grand Rapids, Michigan, 1979), p 68. Abridged from the original edition of 1908, which was published under the title *Quiet Talks with World Winners*.

6 John R. Bisagno, *How to Build an Evangelical Church* (Broadman Press: Nashville, Tennessee, 1971), p 134.

7 *ibid*, p 25.

8 Andrew Kane, *Let There Be Life: The Pain and Joy of Renewal in a Local Church* (Marshall Morgan & Scott: Basingstoke, 1983), p 151.

9 Quoted in C. Peter Wagner, *On the Crest of the Wave: Becoming a World Christian* (Regal Books, California, 1983), p 68.

10 Gene A. Getz, *Sharpening the Focus of the Church* (Moody Press: Chicago, 1974), p 46.

11 Wagner, *Crest of the Wave*, p 89.

12 Patrick Johnstone, *Operation World: A Day-to-Day Guide to Praying for the World* (STL Books: Bromley, Kent, 1986).

11

The Nature of the Church

A new church invited me as guest speaker to their Sunday morning service. It was a pleasant experience. They praised God with enthusiasm and dedication. Then they listened to me, obviously hungry for the message of God. During coffee afterwards there was an opportunity to talk. It was a time of fellowship and genuine concern for one another was evident.

I started a conversation with a young woman of about thirty and just to break the ice I asked whether she had been a Christian for a long time. Only a year, she said. When I asked how she was converted I heard a most interesting story.

'We live just over the road from the school where the church meets. We were young and very idealistic. We joined several clubs and societies that campaign for protection of the environment. But as time went on, we became more and more disappointed. We became critical of the way these clubs were organised. There was such a lot of self-interest and deceit. Our great expectations collapsed like a house of cards. So we just lived from one day to the next, without expecting anything out of life. We were rather sad and discouraged. Our two children could not make up for it, though they gave us a lot of fun.

'On Sundays, we saw people entering the school, but did not know what for. Our eldest son asked one day, "Mum, what are they doing there on Sundays, there are no lessons, are there? And they all look so happy when they arrive. Why is that?" I did not know the answer. My husband said, "I've noticed it as well. They shake hands and kiss as if they had come from the other side of the world. I'd like to know what happens in there."

'I encouraged my husband and one Sunday he went to a service, taking our eldest child as a sort of protection. Nearly three hours later he came back in a totally different mood. He was cheerful, with a new sparkle in his eyes. He told me what had happened, but I did not understand much and brushed it aside. A few days later he was miserable again. So, next Sunday I suggested, "Why don't you go over the road? You look happier when you come out."

'This went on for a few weeks, until I became curious as well. My husband had become more and more cheerful; he was addicted to it! So, one morning I joined him. I only half remember what happened. I did not really understand much of what went on. There was some singing and praying, and all of this was done with a freedom that surprised me. There was some preaching, too, and reading from the Bible. That, however, was not what struck me most. There was something else, something which impressed me deeply. It took hold of me, I sensed its power, but could not say what it was.

'We went there together for a few weeks and started to make friends. We were accepted very easily. Rather unusual, we thought. We were not made to feel as if we had to join at the tail end, as we might have, since we were new to the group.

'Some people visited us and helped us find our way around the Bible. A few months later we were converted and gave our lives to Christ. We believed in Him and thanked Him for taking our sins to the cross. We asked Him to fill us with His Holy Spirit. We prayed and told Him we were looking forward to this in faith. When it happened, we were made new by His Spirit who came to live in us. Little by little we started to understand more about the Scriptures. Now I know it was Someone rather than something who spoke to me that first morning. It was Jesus Christ Himself living among His children, who touched me with His power and presence. He brought about my conversion, He is alive and present. That is why I always enjoy these services: they are meetings with Him.'

As this woman spoke her eyes sparkled with the love of Jesus. Her husband joined us and spoke in the same way. This is the very nature of the church; the risen Lord living among His children. As Eddie Gibbs has pointed out, 'The Church is more than the herald announcing the message, it is a demonstration model which gives credence to the effectiveness of that message.'[1] That explains why these people were attracted to the church: it embodied Jesus Christ Himself. Andrew Kane has observed that 'None of us individually could be to our generation all that Jesus was to the people of his day. What this truth challenged me to believe, however, was that in our corporate identity together we should be all that Jesus was as an individual.'[2] This aspect is often neglected by Christians. We are the body of Christ and He is the Head of the church. That is what the Bible says. The imagery bears a special significance. Although it is true that the Head is in heaven, we need to take seriously the statement that the church on earth is called His body. By this instrument He will be present and make Himself known.

When we look at the church in this way, it will completely change our thinking. Jesus Christ was a blessing to His generation. People flocked to Him; they wanted to be with Him and drank in His words. In His own Person He expressed God's kingdom on earth. He had enemies, but His authenticity exposed them. When the church today starts to follow in His footsteps, the words of Isaiah 58:11 will be fulfilled: 'You will be like a well-watered garden, like a spring whose waters never fail.'

Christian

In the most literal sense of the word, the church is to be Christian. It needs to resemble Him, to express what He stands for, here and now. It lives because of His life; it bears fruit, but cannot produce fruit. Jesus is active through the hands and feet of His church. This central idea is expressed through seven illustrations. There may be more, but these seven are the most relevant. Each one of these examples has an emphasis of its own. They may partially overlap, but we need to consider them all. The order in which we mention them is not the order of significance. Together, they express the relationship between Jesus Christ and His church.

1 Head and body

Jesus Christ is the Head of the church, which is His body. This illustration is found in 1 Corinthians 12, Ephesians 1 and Colossians 1. The Scriptures tell us that the church is not so much an organisation as an organism that draws life and power from its Head. This emphasis is especially strong in Ephesians 4. Jesus also enables the body to function properly and to offer gifts. He makes it grow to full maturity. He is not just the One who provides these abilities, but also the One who oversees the use that is made of them. That is why 1 Corinthians 12 states that the Spirit gives gifts 'to each one, just as he determines' (v 11) with the intention 'that its parts should have equal concern for each other' (v 25). The result is that 'Now you are the body of Christ, and each one of you is a part of it' (v 27). Obviously, a Christian cannot come to this fullness individually. The church in its totality is the body of Christ.

2 Vine and branches

The vine with its branches is another image which Jesus uses to describe our relationship with Him. In John 15, the emphasis is on bearing fruit. Just as moisture in the vine rises up through the branches and into the grapes, so it is with our life in Christ. He made it clear that without Him we can do nothing. That is hard to take. We like to think that we can do almost anything ourselves. With a little effort we are able to produce Christian virtue. But that is impossible in the kingdom of Heaven. The standards by which we judge are of the flesh. They smell of sin. The only thing which is pleasing to God is the fruit that springs from our life in Jesus Christ.

Jesus said, 'If a man remains in me and I in him, he will bear much fruit' (v 5). He accomplishes His work through us. A vine grower in the south of France once told me that when a vine is pruned the sap continues to ooze from the cut. This teaches us, he said, that a branch cannot produce fruit on its own, it has to draw sap from the vine. In the same way, Jesus wants to reveal His character and make His love visible through us. We are branches of the True Vine, joined together with Him, sharing the same life. This fruit-bearing life of Jesus gives pleasure to the Keeper of the vineyard, our Father.

3 High priest and priests

The high priest and the priests are a further illustration. The Old Testament teaches us that Aaron was chosen to lead the priesthood. All priests were set apart for God, but Aaron was the only one who could enter the Holy of Holies to make atonement for the sins of the people. The priests were charged with helping people to approach God. They spoke to God on behalf of the people, and passed on God's blessing to them.

In the New Testament, the church has no priests, or rather all believers are priests. We read this in 1 Peter 2, Revelation 1 and in other scriptures. All believers are expected to go to God for the sake of the people. This is the church's ministry of intercession for the world. Paul says that we need to pray for 'kings and all those in authority' (1 Tim 2:1–2). The church is also authorised to bring God's blessings to the people by proclaiming salvation. It does this in conjunction with the high priest, who has entered the sanctuary after making expiation for sin. His sacrifice was perfect, and valid for all time. The church as a priesthood has the authority to share the blessings that issue from the sacrifice of its high priest.

4 Cornerstone and stones

The cornerstone and the stones that make up the temple are images which appear in Ephesians 2 and elsewhere. The rock on which the church is built is not Peter, but rather the One he confesses, Jesus Christ. This is the only possible foundation for the church (1 Cor 3:11). The temple is a dwelling place for God, where Jews as well as Gentiles are united in His new creation.

In this way, we are built into a large, new body: 'Consequently, you are no longer foreigners and aliens, but fellow citizens with God's people and members of God's household.' In the end, 'the whole building is joined together and rises to become a holy temple in the Lord' (Eph 2:19,21). In Christ we are 'built together.' This also speaks of our closeness with Him. That is why we are no longer far removed, for in Jesus and His church we have grown close to God. We live with God, 'members of God's household,' and He lives in us and with us, 'a dwelling in which God lives' (Eph 2:22).

5 Marriage

Marriage is another image which reveals Jesus' great love for His church. It reflects a love so great that He gave His life for His bride. As expressed in this image, love is wonderful (Eph 5:28–29). When men love their wives, Scripture says, 'He who loves his wife loves himself. After all, no one ever hated his own body, but he feeds and cares for it, just as Christ does the church' (Eph 5:28–29). That is what Christ does with His church today: He nurtures and cherishes it. Like the warmth of the sunshine, Christ's love warms and nurtures His bride. The church comes to life when it begins to understand and enjoy this. It will then reflect His presence and love in the cold darkness of this world.

6 Shepherd and flock

The Shepherd and His flock are an image of the sheep's inclination to wander and get lost, and of the Shepherd's love and
patience with them. John 10 presents a wonderful picture of
this. Jesus Christ is the Shepherd, we are His sheep. He lays
down His life for us, as the Good Shepherd would. Especially
the statement that He is deeply concerned with His sheep
speaks volumes about our relationship with Him. We are precious in His eyes. He leads us and even though we walk
'through the valley of the shadow of death', He is with us (Ps
23:4).

Perhaps you are acquainted with the painting of the
Shepherd carrying a lamb with a broken leg on His back. Even
this is an inadequate illustration of how He faced danger for
us, leads us and finally brings us home. The picture shows the
loving care of the Shepherd. He will find the missing sheep
and add them to the flock, for He has said, 'I have other sheep
that are not of this sheep pen. I must bring them also. They
too will listen to my voice, and there shall be one flock and one
shepherd' (Jn 10:16).

7 The last Adam and the new creation

The last Adam and the new creation, finally, speak of the
wonderful fact that God is not involved with mending what
has gone wrong in the past, but starting something totally
new. When we were born in this world, we were children of
Adam, members of the fallen human race. In Adam all will
die, Scripture says, and nobody disagrees with that. We see it
happening all around us. But another scripture tells us that 'in
Christ all will be made alive' (1 Cor 15:22). The Bible joins
together these two truths. When we are in Adam, we receive
the things that are part of the Fall. When we are in Christ, we
receive the things that belong to the new creation.

This wonderful truth is explained in 1 Corinthians 15.
Although there is a side to it that relates to the future—the

resurrection—it also speaks of bearing the likeness of Christ (1 Cor 15:49). In the second letter to the Corinthians, Paul says, 'Therefore, if anyone is in Christ, he is a new creation; the old has gone, the new has come' (2 Cor 5:17). That is the essence of our relationship with Him: He made everything new as He rose from the dead. He is the firstfruit of God's new creation and we are already part of it. The church therefore foreshadows what God is going to do worldwide.

We need to see afresh what we are as a church and by the grace of God practise what we profess to be. The principle that applies to our personal sanctification also applies here: we are justified in Christ but need to be sanctified in everyday living. The Bible calls us to a holy life and offers several guidelines. We need to be fully aware of who we are and what we have in relation to Jesus Christ before we can start living out that vision according to the standards of the King. We are God's own people, His church, and therefore a 'royal priest-hood' (1 Pet 2:9).

Well-being

Someone has said that the church will prosper when it starts to resemble Christ again. That is a fact, but we need to be careful not to interpret 'prosperity' in the secular way. The so-called 'prosperity evangelism' which is preached today, which teaches that you will prosper as long as you do what Jesus tells you, is an aberration. To have people believe they will get rich because they believe in Christ is against the teaching of Jesus Himself. This was His message:

> Do not be afraid, little flock, for your Father has been pleased to give you the kingdom. Sell your possessions and give to the poor. Provide purses for yourselves that will not wear out, a treasure in heaven that will not be exhausted, where no thief comes near and no moth destroys. For where your treasure is, there your heart will be also (Lk 12:32–34).

So it is important to make clear that biblical prosperity is quite different from the popular idea of prosperity. It is true that people who have been delivered from a chaotic lifestyle, and have begun to live according to Jesus Christ, are better suited to handling money than others. They start to mature, and as a result they often climb up the socio-economic ladder. However, there is no promise of getting on in the world through following Jesus Christ. Our heavenly Father seeks our well-being rather than our prosperity, and sometimes prosperity can jeopardise our well-being. The Bible is full of examples of this.

The biblical idea of well-being involves growth towards a fulfilment of God's plan. Individual Christians, and the church as an assembly of Christians, learn to experience the joy of a God-given destiny, following the example of Jesus Christ Himself. There is a tremendous satisfaction in this.

We are only able to live this new life of service to others through the fullness of the Holy Spirit. That is why the Bible admonishes us always to be full of the Holy Spirit. Krol has pointed out that 'Literally translated, the commission in Ephesians 5:18 runs, "Take care to remain full of the Holy Spirit at all times".'[3] We need to hold out our cup for it to be filled again and again. Life will use up resources, requiring them to be replaced.

It is not just sin that makes us lose the fullness of the Spirit; the mere business of living will drain our strength so that we need to be replenished again. When this flow is maintained, we will be able to share it with others. The more we share, the more we will need to hold out our cup for it to be filled again. This is the secret of well-being in the biblical sense of the word: being filled continually.

When Peter said, 'you have tasted that the Lord is good,' this is what he refers to. The call also comes to us to be transformed into 'a holy priesthood offering spiritual sacrifices acceptable to God through Jesus Christ' (1 Pet 2:3,5). This is our destiny, enabling us to be a blessing to others. This is well-being in the biblical sense.

Spiritual gifts play a significant role here. The subject lies beyond the scope of this book. Spiritual gifts enable a church to do the will of God, and deserve to be treated in their own right and at great length, to forestall misconceptions.

What the church represents

The word 'church' immediately conjures up for most of us the image of a building where believers meet. That was not the case in the New Testament. There:

> the Church is viewed as the Body of Christ—the true laity or people of God (1) organized under one Head, Jesus Christ; (2) equipped by God to perform His functions; (3) ministering to each other; (4) ministering to the world; (5) characterized by a lifestyle of obedience; and (6) reproducing itself individually and corporately.[4]

The church is a new fellowship created by God. He chooses to speak to the world through it. It consists of those who have chosen to live to God's honour and glory. It reflects the kingdom of God. It is not the kingdom itself, but a sign and symbol of it. When we look at the church, we see what God intended for the human race. The believer feels at home in the church. It is a sanctuary where he feels safe. The world is hostile because we belong to Christ, but in church we can relax and be refreshed because we are in the company of our brothers and sisters. We do not need to be fearful. We do not have to prove ourselves or obtain a proficiency certificate.

I remember the opening words of a brother at a Sunday service: 'Make yourself at home. You are a visitor in your own home. This is God's residence and we are His children. Feel free to take off your shoes, if you want to. It might be better not to but you know what I mean. This is home for the children of one Father.' In his straightforward way this man expressed the welcoming nature of fellowship, where we can be ourselves, draw close to one another and to God. He made me think of something Michael Griffiths once said: 'The congregation is the family of God. We are meant to be able to relax, take our shoes off and let our hair down.'[5]

The church is also the Holy Spirit's workshop where God wants to teach and form us. He speaks there through His word and His Spirit. Through our brothers and sisters also He chisels and polishes us. It is the place where He renews lives, heals wounds, chases away loneliness, comforts those in distress and breaks the power of addiction. Scott-Cook has aptly observed that 'The local church is more than a first-aid post or emergency ward with a turnover of patients. It is the extended family of God in which long-term wholeness is realised.'[6]

In the church believers delight in the Lord their God. Attention is paid not only to truth but also to the only true God who lives for all eternity. Praise be to God: He wants to make Himself known, and the church as the assembly of God's children can experience great joy in knowing Him. Christ and His church are joined together in a love relationship. Just as lovers can enjoy one another to the full, the church can enjoy its time together with its Saviour and Lord.

In this context of a loving relationship the church as a whole worships the Lamb on His throne. God wants the church to be continually surprised through discovering different traits of His character. The emphasis has shifted from what He has done to who He is. The church at worship will see more clearly that what He has done reflects His nature and His virtues. It worships Him for who He is and thanks Him for what He did. Its view of Him will determine the church's daily life. It will radiate its enthusiasm for Him. The church is an organism held together by the life that is in it. Paul has expressed it in this way: 'From him the whole body, joined and held together by every supporting ligament, grows and builds itself up in love, as each part does its work' (Eph 4:16).

Whenever Paul speaks about this process of building up the relationship between church members, he zooms in on the themes of faith, hope and love. Faith is focused on Christ. He rose from the dead and represents the new creation. Faith looks forward to the time of complete union with Him. Faith sustains our hope. Even though creation groans under the weight of its present trials, the church knows that these are the pains of childbirth. New life is being given. This hope encourages us to let the love of Christ flow through the church. It does not stop at mystical contemplation, but finds its practical expression in works of love.

What the church says

The church of Christ speaks in the world; that is its God-given obligation and privilege. That does not mean it needs to be involved in world politics. The church would then be on a level with all other organisations which want to make themselves heard in the present system. When Jesus was brought before Pilate, He made it clear that 'My kingdom is not of this world. If it were, my servants would fight to prevent my arrest by the Jews. But now my kingdom is from another place' (Jn 18:36). Therefore, the primary function of the church is not to concern itself with the problems of this world, but rather to be God's messenger of the good news of His love in Christ. The church speaks prophetically of God's justice and the necessity to act accordingly. God will judge this world by the standards He gave it. So both our acts of worship and our pursuit of righteousness are agreeable to Him (Acts 10:35).

The first and foremost task of the church, however, is the proclamation of the gospel. It does this with God's authority, as His spokesman. It is His envoy, His herald in this world. When I preached in Switzerland for the very first time, a prayer meeting was held before the service. People prayed several times that I would proclaim the word 'with authority'. That was new to me. I had not heard that expression used in preparation for preaching, but I understand its importance now. If we are really to communicate what God has to say, we need to be given the authority to do so. When Paul spoke, people were 'cut to the heart' because he spoke with authority (Acts 2:37). He was filled with the Holy Spirit.

Stephen also spoke with authority as he argued with the members of the Synagogue of the Freedmen who 'could not stand up against his wisdom or the Spirit by which he spoke' (Acts 6:10). He spoke as a Spirit-filled defender of the faith. That does not mean that he defeated the opposition. Stephen's adversaries gnashed their teeth and stoned him to death. He paid with his life for speaking with authority. But this was the starting signal for the next stage in God's plan to make known His good news everywhere.

Acts chapter 8 verses 1 and 4 tell us how 'On that day a great persecution broke out against the church at Jerusalem, and all except the apostles were scattered throughout Judea and Samaria. . . . Those who had been scattered preached the word wherever they went.' At that time, it was not just one man who spoke, but the entire church. Believers were scattered by persecutions, but wherever they went, they spread the good news. When we stop and think for a moment, that is a wonderful turn of events. People were driven from their homes, separated from everything dear to them. They were stripped of their possessions and left with the few essentials they could carry. As they passed through different places, people asked questions. 'What has happened to you?' 'Why are you on the run?' 'How is it that you have lost everything?' This is the answer they received from the believers: 'We bring you good news. Jesus of Nazareth is the Messiah. He came and bore our sins. We have been given new life in Him. That is why we are persecuted, but the glad tidings we bring are meant for you as well. Believe in Him and follow Him. He bore your sins, too, and is eager to give you His Spirit. He wants you to share this new life, it's better than anything else on earth.'

Persecuted, they proclaimed peace in Christ; they were poor but proclaimed abundance in Him; strangers on earth, they proclaimed their Father's house has many rooms. They spoke with authority because they were filled with Him. The author of the letter to the Hebrews told them, 'You . . . joyfully accepted the confiscation of your property, because you knew that you yourselves had better and lasting possessions' (10:34).

The church must speak out not only at times of persecution. It must always make its voice heard by the genuineness of its faith and its bond with Christ. I am reminded here of the early beginnings of church planting in a certain town. We made contact with a man who showed up several times, late or early, but always unexpected. Later we learned that his purpose was to find out whether we were only friendly when we were expecting him.

On one occasion he dropped by just as we were about to start a prayer meeting. When we told him, he prepared to leave. But we asked him to stay, and he sat down with us. A prayer meeting might seem rather odd to someone who has not been converted, but we had nothing to hide. When it was over, he asked, 'I heard you pray for a "contact". What do you mean by that?' We explained that we meant someone who was interested in the gospel but had not yet made a decision to follow Christ. A few moments passed, and he replied, 'I guess I am a contact, then.' He was right about that, and a few weeks later, he was converted and as a new-born Christian started to come to our prayer meetings. The first prayer we heard him say was, 'Lord God, give me contacts, people with whom I can share the good news.'

Examples exist to be followed. When a church lives out its relationship with Christ, it does not need to be ashamed. As Jesus lived His life for all the world to see, confirming the word he preached, the church is to live its life. It is authorised to speak and work in this world. When its members do so, filled with God's love, their appeal does not depend on a particular church programme, but rather on the very nature of the church. Dee Brestin speaks of her own experience in this area:

> Many of the people I interviewed received Jesus after attending a Christian seminar, retreat, or evangelistic meeting. How did they happen to attend? They went because a friend invited them. Rarely had they wandered into those events on their own.
>
> Too often we think that we are fulfilling our evangelistic responsibility when our church rents a film or invites a gospel singer. It isn't enough to prepare a three-course candlelit dinner, you must invite the guests.[7]

It is the church, and not just the individual believer in it, that speaks out, and it needs to speak out from a genuine relationship with Christ. Only then will it speak with authority. Christ uses it as His instrument in this world. It follows that witnessing is part of the nature of the church. Some have given in to the temptation to build an ideal church first and start to witness only after that goal has been reached. Terry Virgo reminds us that 'An over-preoccupation with "net-mending" can result in our forgetting what nets are for. We could move on from mending them to embroidering them and hanging them on the walls for decoration. But nets are for catching fish.'[8]

Friendship evangelism receives much emphasis these days. That is fine, as long as we take care not to get stuck in the first stage, that of friendship, and keep the second, that of evangelism, from developing to its full potential. Witnessing is part and parcel of the nature of the church. When this is done in response to New Testament teachings, it will contribute to making the church what it should be.

The same principle is basic to the life of the individual Christian and the life of the church. The more it witnesses about Christ, the more it needs to be purified and dedicated in order to receive spiritual power. The moment it takes its place in the world and begins to speak of its Lord and His rightful insistence on being heard, it must be prepared to be received in a spirit of criticism and scepticism. So it endeavours to receive power. It is in need of strength to witness; as it walks more and more in the way of the Lord, it will receive strength and grow to resemble Him more and more. It will speak out with a deepening compassion for those who are lost. Part of the very nature of the church is to live more and more in accord with God's plan, and to share the life it has received with people who are still in the dark. This kind of witnessing is part of a church's calling.

What the church does

Actions speak louder than words; this principle holds true for the church as well. Its nature needs to be reflected in what it does. Strachan has observed that 'At the heart of the gospel preached and demonstrated by Jesus Christ were concern and compassion for man in every aspect of his life.'[9]

When the church is a true expression of Jesus it will automatically get involved in caring for the whole person. It exists to be of service in this world. This was clearly the case when Paul was recognised by the apostles in Jerusalem as 'an apostle to the Gentiles'. There were no instructions as to his message, for, as Paul tells us, 'All they asked was that we should continue to remember the poor, the very thing I was eager to do' (Gal 2:10). Translated in modern speech, that might read 'In the complexity of modern society, it follows then that social concern and action will form an essential part of the Christian witness.'[10]

Following the example of Christ, there is a caring mission for the church in this world. Although many welfare organisations are already involved in social care, the church is not to dodge its responsibility in this area. Ministering to the whole person is an integral part of the nature and mission of the church. There is no need for us to do what has already been done by others, but a multitude of needs cry out for help.

Hundreds of people have slipped through the social welfare net, and they need our help. There is no outstretched hand for many who grieve. Loneliness, affliction, boredom and a sense of futility need more than a financial allowance. What is needed is a heart, a heart radiating love and care. The church needs to demonstrate the loving heart of Christ.

We must be led by God and be at His disposal to receive His love and pass it on. This needs to start in the church but does not end there: 'Therefore, as we have opportunity, let us do good to all people, especially to those who belong to the family of believers' (Gal 6:10). Christ will lead us and use us as His church as He sees fit. David Prior has aptly observed that 'The love of Jesus frees us to ask others how we may best serve them.'[11]

When love is the motive, there will be no room for rivalry or a spirit of competition. The love song we find in 1 Corinthians 13 describes love at is purest. Love is not self-seeking. All social activity and good works motivated by the desire to enhance the well-being of others must be born of God. God needs to lead us by the power of His Spirit. That will keep the church from losing its sense of balance when setting priorities. If we truly seek the well-being of others, our love will find its expression both in sharing the gospel and in caring for them. People are not just objects to be converted, needing to be ministered to at an early stage so that they might receive the gospel later. On the other hand, experience has taught us that when we feed and clothe them for the rest of their lives without impressing upon them the necessity of salvation in Jesus Christ, we do them a disservice.

In the matter of aid to Third World projects, the local church would do well to build up solid relations with mission and world aid organisations that agree with the basis of our faith. This will ensure that the assistance it provides arrives at the right destination. In the New Testament churches, brothers and sisters took care of each other across national borders. Loving your neighbour begins at home but does not stop there.

The central issue is that we come to see that 'The gospel means we will be concerned about people physically, emotionally and spiritually. We can't separate one from the other and call ourselves compassionate.'[12] It is this compassion which made Jesus unique, and His church needs to have that same compassion. The nature of the church demands that we minister in love and under the leadership of its Head, Jesus Christ.

Practical implications

Our understanding of the nature of the church has certain implications for a church planting ministry. Here are a few practical guidelines:

1 Keeping the ultimate goal in view

We cannot overemphasise the importance of knowing what kind of church we want to build in God's strength. Do we have a clearly defined goal from the start? No architect starts building without a good plan. People involved in church planting often have some ideas, but they have not thought them through. They might intend to copy the church they came from, with some alterations where there were difficulties.

However, it is necessary to reflect deeply in prayer on how to plant a church that is in accordance with God's will. Some might argue that in this way we start with an idealistic picture. This might be true, but we must aim high. After all, God has promised that He will complete His work according to His plan. Christ will present the church 'to himself as a radiant church, without stain or wrinkle or any other blemish, but holy and blameless' (Eph 5:27).

2 Proclamation and power of attraction

Two principles are at work in the spreading of the gospel: the power of the message as it is proclaimed outside the church, and the power of attraction that draws people towards the church. The first is the principle of proclamation, the second is the principle of attraction.

The principle of proclamation was at work when the early church began to spread beyond Antioch, and throughout Asia Minor. In the eighteenth century, one of the spiritual centres from which the gospel went out into the world was the Moravian community in Saxony, planted there by Count von Zinzendorf. H. Berkhof has written:

> The greatest achievement of the Moravian Brethren was perhaps that, more than any other church, they were a mission church and still are today. With an obviousness that puts us all to shame, their history is evidence of the power of the small, or more accurately, the power of faith. At the time of Zinzendorf's death, two hundred missionaries had gone forth from the church of the Brethren.[13]

In this way the gospel spread out over the world and is still spreading today. It goes forth from the church, God's instrument. This activity from within has been discussed in detail in the previous chapter, 'The Church and Its Mission.'

But the church is also intended to attract people towards itself by the very nature of its life. God's message is not only proclaimed by men and women who go out, it is lived out by the local church which has been chosen to reflect God's love, grace and wisdom. When the church becomes what God has intended it to be, it becomes attractive.

The account of the life of the early church in the Acts of the Apostles emphasises the attractive nature of the church. People who were not church members, but watched the church with interest, were affected in several ways by the phenomenon of the church of Jesus Christ. Acts 2 mentions that 'Everyone was filled with awe' (v 43), and that the believers broke bread 'praising God and enjoying the favour of all the people' (v 47). Acts 5:13 records that the believers 'were highly regarded by the people' and Acts 16:5 that 'the churches were strengthened in the faith and grew daily in numbers.' Growth took place as people were drawn to the church. This principle of attraction is effective but should not replace gospel proclamation. They complement one another and both are ordained by God.

3 The glory of God

God is glorified when the church is what He has planned it to be. We need to keep that in view. The church must be pleasing to God so that He may delight in it. In this way, He will be glorified in the midst of a world that is hostile to Him. This is the main reason why the church needs to obey the word of God and be renewed by the power of His Spirit.

It is essential to build the local church in accordance with the plans of the heavenly Architect, and to keep those plans constantly in view.

Notes

[1]   Eddie Gibbs, *I Believe in Church Growth* (Hodder & Stoughton: London, 1985), p 142.

[2]   Andrew Kane, *Let There Be Life: The Pain and Joy of Renewal in a Local Church* (Marshall Morgan & Scott: Basingstoke, 1983), p 16.

[3]   Bram Krol, *Onder Commando: een kompas voor de gemeente van Jezus Christus* (Telos Interlektuur: Arnhem, 1979), p 100.

[4]   James F. Engel and Wilbert Norton, *What's Gone Wrong with the Harvest?* (Zondervan: Grand Rapids, Michigan, 1982), p 137.

[5]   Michael Griffiths, *Cinderella with Amnesia: A Practical Discussion of the Relevance of the Church* (Inter-Varsity Press: London, 1975), p 86.

[6]   Robert Scott-Cook, in *How to Plant Churches* ed Monica Hill (MARC Europe: London, 1984), p 87.

[7]   Dee Brestin, *Finders Keepers* (Hodder & Stoughton: London, 1984), p 147.

[8]   Terry Virgo, *Restoration in the Church* (Kingsway Publications: Eastbourne, 1985), p 98.

9 R. Kenneth Strachan, *The Inescapable Calling* (William B. Eerdmans: Grand Rapids, Michigan, 1968), p 73.

10 *ibid,* p 74.

11 David Prior, *Bedrock: A Vision for the Local Church* (Hodder & Stoughton: London, 1985), p 58.

12 Brestin, *op cit*, p 184.

13 H. Berkhof, *Geschiedenis der Kerk* (Callenbach: Nijkerk, 1955), p 246.

12

The Church as the Answer

'Before I became a Christian, I had no goal in life and did not know what to do with myself. I did not know the reason for my existence, where I was heading or where I came from. But all of that has changed. Now I have a goal to live for and lots of friends who share that goal.'

The speaker was a young Christian describing what he found when he turned to Christ and joined His church. The New Testament teaches us clearly that people who are born again are not orphans in the kingdom of God. They are born into God's family.

When Paul sends Onesimus back to his master, he says that he 'became my son while I was in chains' but returns 'no longer as a slave, but better than a slave, as a dear brother . . . in the Lord' (Philem 10,16). That is the character of the new relationship. Onesimus has been taken into God's family. In a similar way the new converts in Thessalonica were not left behind on a spiritual island. They 'joined Paul and Silas' (Acts 17:4). They were accepted into the group and received from it what they needed to grow, as babies born into a family. The church is God's answer to a multitude of human needs. It does not only proclaim that Christ is the answer; it is itself God's answer.

The value of the church

Church planting evangelism is God's strategy, following the

New Testament example. It is also God's answer to fundamental human needs. We have not been created for solitude. We have a need for love, recognition and appreciation. Our Creator has put these natural, human desires in our heart. The world exploits and perverts these needs, but in the church God has prepared a place where human needs can be satisfied in a way that glorifies Him. God has equipped us with spiritual gifts that enable members of His church to minister to one another in order to experience the mutual fulfilment of their needs. Salvation is more than remission of sins and being rescued from our lost state. It includes our development into balanced individuals, learning to live to the glory of God. The church is His instrument for salvation. It follows that we are to proclaim God's message in a way that gives results according to God's intentions: 'We must always ask just one question: Are the methods getting God's results?'[1]

This question leads us into church growth and church planting. We are not born homeless; God has prepared a 'nest' for us when we come to life by faith in Christ. That nest means for a young Christian the same thing as it would mean for a fledgeling. Let us beware, therefore, that the church does not miss its goal by becoming an institution. What was first a movement of warm affection then becomes a cold monument to the lost glory of earlier and better days. All that is then left is an empty shell, divorced from any inner experience. True Christianity, however, 'rooted in God's revelation and a highly developed sense of membership in the body of Christ, sees Christian truth touching every area of a person's life.'[2]

The church is the place where we discover our Christian destiny in all its fullness. It is the community where we can drop our masks and be ourselves. And what a relief that is! This is how the church becomes God's answer to our human need to find our true identity: 'We shall be real people, living a total life but with the mark of authenticity our world desperately needs to see.'[3] The local church is not an end in itself but an instrument in God's hand with which He wants to be active. Kenneth Strachan has said that:

> It is helpful to remember that the local congregation exists for three purposes: (1) to nourish and support the spontaneous witness of its members who are scattered strategically throughout the community; (2) to furnish that additional and authoritative declaration of the gospel and its implications for all of life which is not possible to the individual members; and (3) to make visible through its communal life, fellowship, and service a foreseeing of the Kingdom of God, thus supporting the message preached.[4]

The more we think about the church, the more splendidly it unfolds before us as an expression of God's wisdom. It is God's intention 'that now, through the church, the manifold wisdom of God should be made known to the rulers and authorities in the heavenly realms' (Eph 3:10). The local church has been chosen to be a symbol of this. From the world's point of view, God is a thousand miles away, but through the church, the world can get to know Him.

Needs answered

The church has a purpose, not only for the world outside, but also for the Christians within it. For them it is a place of refuge where they can find peace and satisfaction, and grow to their full potential. In a lecture on the subject of missionary tensions, Marion Ashton has stated that 'one of the commonest reasons for missionaries having problems is that in some areas of their lives they are deprived of their basic needs.' She then gives a short list of four emotional needs: 'The need for significance. The need for belonging. The need for purpose. The need for love—given and received.'[5]

As you read this, you might think, 'That is true, it is the price that a missionary must pay for his ministry and vocation.' Man or woman, the missionary has to leave the home church and start from nothing in a foreign land, cut off from the fulfilment of needs for which the church provides. It is

God's wish that in His church we grow to be balanced, mature Christians, and have our needs met by belonging to His church. Because we have a place and function in the church, we are important, every one of us.

I would like to list five needs for which the church provides. My list is by no means exhaustive, but it shows that the church is one of God's answers to human requirements. We are not called to lead the life of Robinson Crusoe, in solitary exile on a spiritual island. God's church is a place we can come home to.

A challenge to our faith

Everyone needs to have faith. By faith we are born again and receive forgiveness of sins. But faith is like a muscle: it becomes slack when it is not used. Effort is necessary to keep it functioning properly. A Christian needs to be challenged regularly so that his faith is exercised.

In our local church we are confronted with such challenges. Brothers and sisters go through hard times. They need help, but human resources are lacking. This leads to a state of emergency where people do not just pray, they cry out to God. Faith is put under tension, like a bow string. The more the bow is bent, the further the arrow will fly. And when our prayers are made tense by need, they will soar like arrows straight to God. The psalms are full of such prayers, and God answers them in wonderful ways. In the church we can take part in that struggle together by sharing such experiences with one another. God often confronts the whole church with faith-challenging situations. This is especially so when a group of Christians sets about executing what God has commissioned them to do, in obedience to Him. A church meets opposition when it comes out into the open and proclaims that its Master has risen from the dead, and now lives and reigns. The devil moves into action and we need to marshal prayer and active faith against his attacks.

This is one of the reasons why we always need to look ahead to what God is going to do. Our faith is built on who He is and we are saved by what He has done. But we must not always be looking back. God wants to act today as well. There is a danger in praying for revival if we only pray for something that is past instead of something new. Renewal is what we need to pray for. When we focus our attention on the future, we can expect God to do something new. The Bible is filled with promises. God is going to do great things today. He will 'pour water on the thirsty land, and streams on the dry ground' (Is 44:3). He says, 'Call to me and I will answer you and tell you great and unsearchable things you do not know' (Jer 3:3). The Bible is crammed full of such 'great and unsearchable things' and if you like to believe that those promises were meant only for ancient Israel, my reply is, 'Do we not believe in the God of Israel? Has He changed? Have not these things been given as examples to build us up?' We are privileged and obliged to encourage one another, and the place where this happens is the church: 'Therefore encourage one another and build each other up, just as in fact you are doing' (1 Thess 5:11).

The church is the right place for prayer and intercession. When we learn to minister to one another in this way, we receive a sense of expectancy. Our faith enters into action and the cobwebs of doubt are blown away. Everything becomes fresh and green again because faith is active. Being together in the church gives us the opportunity to warn one another against 'hitch-hiker's disease'. People who suffer from that illness just stand by the side of the road, hoping for a lift, but never turn around to look for stopping cars. They do not believe a car will stop. Half-hearted prayers are not pleasing to God. We need to be like David and say, 'Morning by morning I lay my requests before you and wait in expectation' (Ps 5:3).

I am reminded of the time when we first decided to plant a new church, a short distance from the mother church. We could not find a house to accommodate the team ready to make a start. The need was urgent. There was much praying and searching, and we became more and more desperate. Our team members were due to arrive at the beginning of the following week. On the Saturday before, I went down on my knees and prayed an urgent prayer. Then I browsed through my Bible, to pass the time. God spoke to me through John 14:12-13, 'I tell you the truth, anyone who has faith in me will do what I have been doing. He will do even greater things than these, because I am going to the Father. And I will do whatever you ask in my name, so that the Son may bring glory to the Father.'

As I was reflecting on those 'greater things,' I asked myself, 'What does it mean?' Jesus worked with a team, and we were about to do the same. He had a team of twelve; should we set out with a team of thirteen? While I was thinking and waiting upon God for an answer, it became clear to me that the 'greater things' were not meant for the individual Christian, but for the church as a whole.

The passage also said, 'I will do whatever you ask in my name.' So I knelt down again and asked in Christ's name for a house. My heart was filled with peace and joy while I prayed. I received the certainty that I had already received what I had prayed for (1 Jn 5:15). It was a wonderful experience; my heart overflowed with praise and thanksgiving. During the service the following day I announced that God had given us a house. Many came up to me afterwards and asked for the address. I was in a tight spot there, I had nothing to tell them! The church became closely involved with the course of events. When I was strolling down the street the following day, a man came up to me and said, 'I believe you are the person looking for a house in this neighbourhood. I might have one for you!'

I was dumbfounded. What had happened? That same weekend an old lady had died. She had been in intensive care at the hospital for over a year. Her son had decided not to rent out her home as long as she lived, even though she was incurably ill. You can imagine the joy when I broke the news. I telephoned several church members; I could not wait until the following Sunday. We rejoiced in the God of our salvation, who still comes to our rescue. We found that a joy shared is a joy multiplied. Such experiences have their rightful place in the church. God receives praise and worship from a multitude of people, and we build up, inspire and encourage one another.

A meaningful life

The church helps us to live life with a purpose. By faith we have become children of God. The Bible says that 'we are God's workmanship, created in Christ Jesus to do good works, which God prepared in advance for us to do' (Eph 2:10). That means that God has a plan for our lives. We are made anew in Christ Jesus. In Him we are the new creation, in Him we live and have our being from the moment we are born again. He enables us to take our place in God's new order and get to know God's intentions for our lives.

Each one of us is involved in discovering God's new direction for our lives. Paul makes this clear when he states that we are all one in Christ: 'But to each one of us grace has been given as Christ apportioned it' (Eph 4:7). This is not the grace by which we are saved, but the grace to serve. What is meant here is the gifts of grace, granted to each one of us. It follows that the ultimate goal is to serve God and each other. At the point of conversion He endows us with a specific ability to fulfil the purpose He has in mind for us. All of this happens within the church; it is the place where gifts are discovered and given room to function.

A question that concerns many Christians is: How do I know which gifts I have been given? The answer lies within the church. The individual Christian does not stand alone in the matter of discovering his gift; brothers and sisters surrounding him often notice a gift as soon as it begins to develop. They are quick to recognise the way God uses a person to bring blessing in a particular situation. They can help him to see that God has given him a gift and wants him to use it. In this way, the church lives up to its calling.

This recognition of gifts could be on an impressive scale, as in the case of the early missionaries in Acts 13. The church as a whole recognised the mission to be of God and let them go out after a period of prayer and fasting. But it works on a smaller scale as well, in everyday life, when brothers and sisters of our church recognise that God has given us not only a mission to accomplish but the necessary abilities as well. We offer assistance to one another in finding out the will of God and in so doing we discover our life's direction. We are made aware that our life is of value; the church recognises this and confirms us in it.

The church will also be there when things go wrong, when our wishes do not match our abilities and we end up like square pegs in a round hole. In a climate of loving care, with brothers and sisters ready to serve one another in a joint effort to find God's goal, help can be found in the fellowship. It is important that the seed principle applies in our lives. Jesus said, 'I tell you the truth, unless an ear of wheat falls to the ground and dies, it remains only a single seed. But if it dies, it produces many seeds' (Jn 12:24). This is precisely the reason why the church can bring us to live a meaningful life. We can only truly belong in the church through the grave. When we recognise that we have died with Christ, we are set free to live for God. In this awareness of the newness of life in Christ, members of a church can help one another to find their Creator's goal for their lives and press towards it. This opens up a vista on eternity and gives a new dimension to our lives. In John's words, 'The world and its desires pass away, but the man who does the will of God lives for ever' (1 Jn 2:17). Where do we find a 'club' equal to that?

Solid relationships

There is another fundamental need that we all share: having friends who love you, friends you can rely on, people who miss you when you are not there. Terry Virgo has said something striking about the depth of that relationship: 'It is because we feel ourselves to be friends of God that we are freed to be friends with one another.'[6] This is the foundation of all relationships within the church. It is significant that Paul in Ephesians 5 draws a parallel between being drunk and being filled with the Holy Spirit. People who have had too much to drink make good friends. They indulge in frivolous talk, have lost their sense of inhibition, pat each other on the back and say things they would never say normally. They have shaken off the restraints that go with sobriety and have the courage to show themselves as they are. Their friendship is based on being together, and being drunk together.

Being born again, we have entered into a relationship with our heavenly Father and with each other. The agent that cements our friendship is the fullness of God's Spirit. Living under His influence makes us into a group of people who belong to one another and take delight in one another's company. Speaking from experience, Terry Virgo has written that 'Drunkenness through alcohol, which often released and apparently enriched my old friendships, was replaced by a new Holy Spirit drunkenness which led to laughter, joy and freedom among Christians.'[7]

'We are all baptised by one Spirit into one body,' says the Scripture (1 Cor 12:13). On this basis we belong together. This unity is visible not only in exuberance, but through fellowship in times of hardship and suffering: 'Rejoice with those who rejoice; mourn with those who mourn' (Rom 12:15). Fellowship is a characteristic of the church of Christ. It is based on the *koinonia* principle of being givers and takers of God's grace. It implies that together we live out what it means to be God's own people. The value of these relationships is revealed when times are hard. In this area Scripture admonishes us, 'Brothers, if someone is caught in a sin, you who are spiritual should restore him gently' (Gal 6:1). Michael Griffiths has explained that 'restore' in this context means 'mend', 'That is, bring that member back into proper articulation with all the other members.'[8]

When we start helping each other in this way, and fulfil God's purpose for His church, relationships will develop that are not easily broken. I have heard many people admit that they enjoy closer relationships with their brothers and sisters in the Spirit than with their natural family. Sharing the same life forges us together. In an article entitled 'Open to God— Closed to the Church', Leslie K. Tarr reviews a study of Donald C. Posterski about the role of the church in youth ministry. He writes, 'Young people today place a high value on friendship, the survey revealed. . . .In opting for friendship as a priority, young people expressed indifference for institutions, including the church. Paradoxically, Posterski states, they appeared to be "open to God—closed to the church".' He concludes that 'Organisational structures are being pushed aside by the appeal of significant relationships.'[9]

It is obvious that a church doing the will of God, and based on New Testament guidelines, answers a legitimate need, not only of the young, but of us all.

A sense of belonging

The need to belong is closely related to the need for solid relationships. Naturally, we have closer contact with a limited number of people. The same is true in the church. We cannot be on intimate terms with a large number of people. We are more attracted to some people than to others, and some God-given gifts are better suited to one than to another. So we have a general sense of belonging to the whole family while developing deep relationships with a smaller number of people.

Even Jesus had a closer relationship with three of His disciples—John, James and Peter—than with the others. This was not at the expense of His love for the others.

That is how it should be in the church. Derek and Nancy Copley have observed that 'Adam and Eve had a deep sense of *belonging*—to each other and to God. They knew they were *accepted*.'[10] God also intends the church to enjoy belonging to Him. To this end we have been restored. God's ripped and torn creation is restored in Christ. We belong to Him and to each other. To belong is an essential part of life in the church, and answers a deep need of the human heart. It means that 'When someone is added they are not added to the back of the queue—they help make up the circle.'[11]

Andrew Kane tells about Tertullian, 'one of the early church fathers, . . .who recorded the following testimony of unbelievers to the saints, "See how these Christians love one another".'[12] This is the heart of the Christian principle of belonging to the church. Belonging is not based on natural attraction or preference, its foundation is that we are accepted in Jesus Christ. We belong to Him and, in consequence, we belong to one another. When we really experience this, we become enthusiastic supporters of our own church; more fervent than football fans could ever be!

A knowledge of God

Belonging to a church gives direction and purpose to our lives. We belong by the grace of Christ, who has forgiven our sins. The past has been put under the blood of Christ: 'So from now on we regard no one from a worldly point of view' (2 Cor 5:16). We are free to progress towards a new life, a new future and a new destination. What a joyful prospect! Before that happens, it is good to have a proper understanding of how this works, 'in order that you may know the hope to which he has called you' (Eph 1:18).

This is why churches have Bible studies. The Book that

makes God known is vital to the life of the church and each member's personal experience of that life. It gives understanding and wisdom. It contains the truth. It explains the beginning and the end of all things. It gives a clear picture of the truth and helps us discern the powers and authorities in the invisible world. It makes us alert to dangers on the road, and teaches us how to walk along it. It is God's manual for our lives. The Bible teaches us about God's revelation of Himself; His works and actions, both past and future.

The more often we listen to God's word, the better we understand Him. His guidelines will become part of our thinking. Jesus said that 'everyone who hears these words of mine and puts them into practice is like a wise man who built his house on the rock' (Mt 7:24).

To have built our life on a foundation strong enough to withstand storms is a wonderful certainty. When you live by the Bible, you do not need to go through life armed with all sorts of theories and resources to prove yourself. You know where you come from, where you are heading and why you are where you are now. This gives a sense of satisfaction and security. The church is the place where we can be of assistance and acquire a better understanding of the word of God. Nobody has a monopoly on wisdom, but we have all received the Holy Spirit and He enables us to build each other up in our most holy faith. The Bible is full of verses that encourage us to build up, inspire, encourage, protect and admonish one another. This is achieved through using the Bible, 'in your light we see the light' (Ps 36:9).

The knowledge we acquire by reading the word of God answers a deep need. Ever since he was chased out of Eden, man has been searching frantically for the meaning of his existence—and has found it in God's word. An experienced Christian in the Netherlands was responsible for a small ferry service across the River Issel. When a few people had boarded the ferry, he used to ask, 'Are you looking for Paradise as well?' He knew that most people did not just want to cross the river. They were longing for something better, if only at a subconscious level. The church is God's instrument to show the way to salvation and restoration. Although it is not Paradise itself, it points the way. In the meantime, it is called to be a sign and symbol of the coming kingdom of God.

Jesus Christ has risen from the dead, so everything is possible. He is the Head of the church and able to do infinitely more than we pray for or know. We can rely on His promise, 'I will build my church' (Mt 16:18). Anyone who joins the army that fights to achieve this under His leadership, helps to provide an answer to human needs and is part of the winning team. Hallelujah!

Notes

[1] James F. Engel and Wilbert Norton, *What's Gone Wrong with the Harvest?* (Zondervan: Grand Rapids, Michigan, 1982), p 157.

[2] John Wimber, *Power Evangelism: Signs and Wonders Today* (Hodder & Stoughton: London, 1985), p 82.

[3] Donald Llewelyn Roberts, *The Practicing Church* (Christian Publications: Harrisburg, Pennsylvania, 1981), p 34.

[4] R. Kenneth Strachan, *The Inescapable Calling* (William B. Eerdmans: Grand Rapids, Michigan, 1968), p 87.

[5] Derek and Nancy Copley, *Building with Bananas: People Problems in the Church* (Paternoster Press: Exeter, 1984), pp 53–54.

[6] Terry Virgo, *Restoration in the Church* (Kingsway Publications: Eastbourne, 1985), p 73.

[7] *ibid*, p 70.

[8] Michael Griffiths, *Cinderella with Amnesia: A Practical Discussion of the Relevance of the Church* (Inter-Varsity Press: London, 1975), p 63.

[9] Leslie K. Tarr, 'Open to God—Closed to the Church', *World Evangelization* vol 13 (December 1986): p 13.

[10] Copley, *op cit*, p 57.

[11] Virgo, *op cit*, p 102.

[12] Andrew Kane, *Let There Be Life: The Pain and Joy of Renewal*

in a Local Church (Marshall Morgan & Scott: Basingstoke, 1983), pp 98–99.

Appendix: How to Use the Bridge Illustration Effectively

Military equipment is very useful for battle when used properly, but used clumsily, it might be positively dangerous. The same is true of spiritual warfare. Some resources are very useful, if used in the right way. But mistakes can have unfortunate results, possibly to the extent of putting people off.

One of the dangers is that people get hardened to the gospel. They think they have understood it and believe they do not need it. In actual fact they have no real understanding of what the gospel is about. When they are approached again some time later, they tell us not to bother explaining it again, 'I've heard it before and know what it is all about.' All our ammunition has been used too soon, without any result. That is a mistake we should try to avoid. The following guidelines might help you to obtain the best possible results when presenting the gospel. I consider the bridge illustration to be a most effective resource for communicating the basic truths of the gospel. I do not quite remember how it came to be invented, but it has been used by many people. Some have been very successful in applying this as an explanatory method, others have used it without quite reaching their objectives.

In the Belgian Evangelical Mission we have developed a presentation that we call the 'five evenings' approach. We make use of the bridge illustration on the fourth evening. A more detailed account of the 'five evenings' has been given in Chapter 4. Our theme for the fourth evening is 'man'. The bridge illustration serves to explain who man is and what his position is in relation to God. When done properly, it can touch people's hearts and set them thinking seriously about themselves and their relationship with God and eternity. Naturally, not everyone is converted as a result, but many will be challenged, to the point of confessing their faith in Christ as Lord and Creator.

A few preliminary points need to be made before we go over this method of explanation step by step.

1 We use this illustration with people who have been prepared for a gospel presentation. For three evenings prior to this we talk with them and show them biblical principles. We do not reach for this weapon at a first encounter.

2 We need to let the Bible speak for itself during this presentation. The word of God is the sword of the Spirit and God uses it to convince people. Hebrews 4:12 applies here: it is 'a double-edged sword' and 'penetrates even to dividing soul and spirit, joints and marrow; it judges the thoughts and attitudes of the heart.' God's word succeeds where our words fall short.

3 We should beware of compromise and watering down the truth when the Bible makes uncomfortable reading. One of the strengths of the bridge illustration is that it clearly shows us to be sinners unable to contribute positively to our own salvation. This is a painful and humbling discovery for people, so we might be tempted to soften the blow and present the gospel in a more acceptable way. However, that is making improper use of our weapons. We should beware of adapting the truth, however slightly, in order to avoid inflicting pain. We are to speak the truth lovingly, but love does not imply twisting the truth.

A good start

For the bridge illustration to be used effectively, we need to agree to spend some time discussing it with the person or persons we are trying to reach. The best way is to use it as part of a series of 'five evenings' that several people attend. Otherwise, simply ask if you could spend some time together with your contact to explain the gospel in a clear and graphic way. Start by taking a piece of paper to draw the illustration. This will make a greater impact than ready-made printed material. Your message will come over as something that is natural and straight from the heart, rather than a prepared message with an artificial sound.

Making things clear

Start with a vertical axis and draw a horizontal on top of it in the shape of an inverted L. Above the horizontal line write 'God'.

God

Then ask, 'Suppose there is a God, a Supreme Being who rules everything, what should His personality and character be like?' Most people will answer: 'He should be good, just, loving, honest and compassionate.' We could ask questions and come up with some more ideas: He should have independent life, be holy, be pure. Write this list down under the horizontal line, as follows:

God

good
just
loving
honest
compassionate
living
holy
pure
. . .

Confirm that these are good answers and then ask, 'Shouldn't we be like that as well? Perhaps not to perfection, as God is, but shouldn't we be good, just, loving and honest as well? Do you agree?' The purpose of this is to make people aware of human frailty and man's failure to come up to God's standard.

Continue by drawing a second vertical axis with a horizontal line on top. Above it write 'man'.

man   *God*

good
just
loving
honest
compassionate
living
holy
pure
. . .

Next suggest exploring the Bible together to discover what God says about man and the state he has come to be in. First turn to Isaiah 59:1–2 and ask your friend to read it out loud. The idea is to get the other person involved. When he reads it himself, your friend will grasp the meaning faster and it will take root more deeply. You need to give a brief explanation, preferably by asking questions. 'What is it that separates men from God, according to this scripture?', or, put differently, 'What is the effect of sin on our relationship with God?' Add the key words 'separation' and 'sin' on the diagram, putting 'sin' in the gap between the vertical lines. This illustrates separation and its cause. Then write 'separation' under the caption 'man'.

man		*God*
Isaiah 59:1–2		
separation		*good*
		just
	sin	*loving*
		honest
		compassionate
		living
		holy
		pure
		. . .

Develop the left side of your drawing by reading a few Bible verses, each time writing down a key word that illustrates the state of man. After Isaiah 59, turn to Romans 3:23: 'all have sinned'. Make clear there are no exceptions; God deals with people without personal considerations. Turn to Romans 6:23 next and focus on 'the wages of sin is death'. Explain that wages are something we earn, something we are entitled to. It is often necessary to explain the meaning of death at this point, to forestall some of the current misunderstandings in this area. Start by pointing out that physical death is a separation of body and soul, which does not mean that we cease to exist. In colloquial language we would say 'He gave up the ghost' or 'He breathed his last.'

Just as there is physical death, so there is spiritual death. There is the same underlying idea of separation, but this time it is between man and God. Although we are separated from God, we go on existing, but we are not alive. Cut flowers will retain their perfume and colour, but have died because they have been severed from their roots. Separated from the very source of life, they merely exist. Physical death is an undeniable reality as a result of our spiritual death.

Go on to Hebrews 9:27 and focus on judgement. This scripture says that there is a direct link between judgement and the fact that everyone must die and give an account of himself.

In the end, the drawing looks like this:

man		*God*
Isaiah 59:1–2		
separation		good
Romans 3:23		just
all have sinned	*sin*	loving
Romans 6:23		honest
death		compassionate
Hebrews 9:27		living
judgement		holy
		pure
		. . .

Probably it is wise at this point to stop for a moment and inquire whether everything so far is clear. We need to be careful not to lose sight of the general drift of our conversation, but must be prepared for questions along the way. Sometimes the questions jump the gun; the best thing to do then is to say you will give an answer later, and suggest you continue with the presentation.

The time has now come to explain that in every age and every civilisation, man is occupied with constructing bridges to get to the other side. Often this happens unconsciously; man is searching for the happiness he has been destined to know. He chases after it frantically. Even when he is looking in the wrong direction, there is something within him that compels him to struggle towards God.

Some people construct bridges of their own: a noble character, love for their neighbour, helping the Third World, care of the environment, and so on. Others still construct bridges of religion: going to church, praying, social involvement, and doing good works. It is a good policy to find out at this stage where your friend stands and which bridges he might have constructed. This enables us to understand his particular situation. You could sketch in a few of those bridges on the illustration. Write down a few possible names, leaving open the question of 'What is your particular bridge? How do you try to get to the other side?' It might take some time to get an answer, but a few moments of silence at this point in the conversation might be appropriate. It is a sign that the other person is doing some thinking of his own and is taking it all in. Do not hurry; wait patiently, and put down in one single word the name of the bridge your friend has indicated.

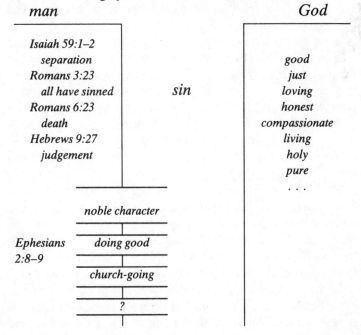

When you have drawn these bridges and pointed out their significance—man's attempts to clear the way to his destination and his Creator—give your friend Ephesians 2:8–9 to read. It is of vital importance that these verses be understood correctly. You have to make clear that human effort amounts to nothing, for it is a 'no through road', a dead end. These bridges, as the drawing shows, do not reach the other side. Whatever we try, we cannot quite reach. Be frank about this and cross out all the bridges with a few firm strokes. Let this sink in for a few moments and pray that God might convince your friend in his heart by the power of the Holy Spirit of the utter hopelessness of his state.

Many people ask at this point, 'How do I get to the other side?' If so, you have a wonderful opportunity to continue your presentation. Some of the answers you gave in the course of these 'five evenings' might have surprised your friend. So you say, 'I'll answer that next week when we meet again.' The idea is that, rather than respond to an emotional reaction, you would give people the opportunity to let the truth of their lost state and inability to work their own salvation sink in to the deepest recesses of their minds. The extra week is, in particular, spent in praying that the Holy Spirit would do His work of conviction in their hearts, as is shown in John 16:8–9.

Then suggest that people keep this drawing and put it somewhere within reach to remind them as the week goes by. When you meet a week later, ask them for it and go on from there.

In some cases, your course of action will not be so clear. You then need to adhere more closely to the general scheme. Suppose you are not asked the question, 'How do I get to the other side?' You will then have to ask it yourself, since it touches the heart of your message. What follows is the answer to that question.

You want to show that, since it was not possible for us to make peace with God, in His infinite goodness God made His peace with us. The Word became flesh; Jesus Christ became flesh. He came down to us, revealed the Father to us and died to save us from sin. Indicate that by drawing a horizontal line linking God's side with man's side across the gap. In the gap write 'John 1:14' and 'John 3:16'.

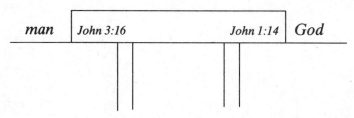

Jesus Christ not only bridged the gap; He came to take away our sin and in so doing take away the cause of separation. It is important to explain this thoroughly. Jesus was not just an example showing people how to live; He was 'the lamb of God that takes away sin'. That explains why the cross was necessary: Jesus died on behalf of others. We cannot restore our relationship with God without Jesus Christ's sacrificial death. Express that graphically by adding a vertical line which crosses the horizontal, so that the cross is seen to emerge and 'cross out' sin. It shows God's wonderful redemptive plan; in His wisdom He has cleared the way for us to return to Him. In the vertical column write 'John 1:29'. While your friend is reading it out loud, add 'John 19:30' to indicate that Christ has accomplished the work He came down to us to accomplish. Put down Romans 6:23 as well. This verse has come up earlier, but the emphasis then was on 'the wages of sin is death.' Now it shifts on to the latter half of the verse: 'the gift of God is eternal life in Christ Jesus our Lord.'

So, by means of this drawing, you are explaining the meaning of justification by faith. Christ took sin upon Himself and gives us His righteousness when we come to Him in faith. Jesus 'was delivered over to death for our sins and was raised to life for our justification' (Rom 4:25). The finished drawing looks like this:

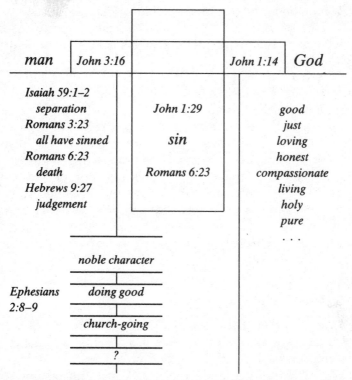

Once you have given the whole presentation, the time has come for you to ask your listener where he would put himself in the drawing. More often than not, he will point to a spot somewhere in the middle, on the bridge. That probably indicates his uncertainty about where he stands in his relationship with Christ, as well as his curiosity to know more about it. Should that be the case, we could explain that he is either on one side, or on the other, but that all are invited to come over to God's side, through Christ. This is the time when an invitation is made for him to give his heart and life to Christ through a simple act of faith—to repent of his sins and humbly ask for the Lord's favour to be adopted as His child. When we have brought someone before the Lord in prayer, it is a good idea

to read some verses together—1 John 5:12-13, for example—
to let the Scriptures strengthen him in his faith. It goes without
saying that the appropriate arrangements must be made for
pastoral follow-up.

When someone puts himself on the left side of the horizontal axis, the same invitation could be made to come to God by
the route He has opened up for us.

When people tell us they are on the right side of the axis,
you ask how they know: 'Why do you put yourself right
there?' They might be Christians, confirming their faith in the
Lord by means of the drawing. You should not rule out that
possibility; however, some people fool themselves into a false
sense of security. They claim to be on the right side but cannot
tell why. You need to see through this and help them to come
to God with a sincere heart in the one way He has prepared for
us in Jesus Christ.

Final words of advice

If you use this method as a tool for presenting the gospel, you
would do well to keep notes about the presentation you have
given. How did it go? What kind of conversation did you
have? Where did it possibly go wrong? Which arguments were
put forward against it? How could you have avoided these
obstacles? What could be done better next time?

The idea is to improve your skills and to learn from failure
as well as success. In this way you give the Holy Spirit the
opportunity to teach you how to be more useful next time.
This is at the heart of Paul's advice: 'Do your best to present
yourself to God as one approved, a workman who does not
need to be ashamed and who correctly handles the word of
truth' (2 Tim 2:15).